Tipping the Balance

A study of non-take up of benefits in an inner city area

Carolyn Davies
Department of Health and Social Security

Jane Ritchie
Social and Community Planning Research

LONDON: HER MAJESTY'S STATIONERY OFFICE

© *Crown copyright 1988*
First published 1988

ISBN 0 11 321147 3

Contents

		Page
PART I THE CONTEXT		
Chapter 1	**The starting point**	1
1.1	Introduction	1
1.2	The benefits	1
1.3	A review of previous take up research	3
1.4	The focus of the present study	7
Chapter 2	**The study design**	8
2.1	Hackney: an inner city area	8
2.2	The sample of non-claimants	9
2.3	The four stages of the study	11
2.4	A profile of the eligible non-claimants	13
Chapter 3	**Changes in claiming behaviour**	18
3.1	Introduction	18
3.2	Changes after nine months	19
3.3	Changes after two years	26
PART II A TEST OF THE KERR THRESHOLD MODEL		
Chapter 4	**The threshold model**	33
4.1	Introduction	33
4.2	The Kerr threshold model	33
4.3	The application of the model in the present study	35
4.4	Testing the model: the results	38
4.5	Failed cases	43
4.6	Summary	46
PART III CROSSING THE THRESHOLD TOWARDS A CLAIM		
Introduction	**The balance of forces**	49
Chapter 5	**The negative forces: factors which discourage claiming**	51
5.1	Lack of perceived need	51
5.2	Uncertainty about entitlement	56
5.3	Beliefs and feelings about the claim process	60

		Page
5.4	Unstable circumstances	65
5.5	Negative attitudes towards income support	65
5.6	Summary	66

Chapter 6	**The positive forces: factors which encourage claiming**	67
6.1	Introduction	67
6.2	Increased awareness of need	67
6.3	Personalised information, advice and encouragement	68
6.4	Changing attitudes towards the benefit system: the interactive effect of positive influences	72

Chapter 7	**Summary and implications**	75
7.1	Main findings of the research	75
7.2	Implications for the proposed system of income related benefits	77
7.3	Implications for promoting take up	77

Appendices   81

References   169

This research study was carried out jointly by Carolyn Davies of the Department of Health and Social Security and Jane Ritchie of Social and Community Planning Research. It was funded by the Department of Health and Social Security. The opinions expressed in the report are those of the authors and do not necessarily reflect the views of the Department.

We should like to express here our gratitude to those who have contributed to this research. We are particularly indebted to Scott Kerr, who acted as a consultant to the study in its early stages, and provided advice about its design. We have greatly appreciated the help and encouragement given by other members of the Social Research Branch of DHSS, in particular by Hazel Houghton, Patrick Hennessy, Alison Matthews, Carol Tozer and George Hipwell. The careful contribution of three students, Susan Taylor, Simon Robinson and Philippa Williams, who worked on the study during short term placements, should also receive some note.

Within SCPR, a number of people have had an important input into the design and conduct of the study. We would particularly like to acknowledge the contribution made by Jennifer Waterton, whose sound advice on some of the statistical aspects of the study, went far beyond her specific brief. Special thanks are also due to Judith England, a co-author of the Hackney Benefit Study, who helped with the research in its early stages; to Jackie Hewlett, Mary Osborne, Jo Perriam and the interviewers who patiently battled with the complexities of the survey during its operation stages; and, perhaps most important, to the families in Hackney who gave up their time to be interviewed on two separate occasions.

Finally we would like to mention the help given by the London Borough of Hackney. We thank them for the commissioning of the original research and for allowing the follow-up study to be undertaken.

PART I

The Context

The starting point

1.1 Introduction

This report is concerned with explanations of non-take up of means tested benefits. Its purpose is to build on evidence from previous research and to further define the processes and influences affecting claiming behaviour. Since the early seventies, research studies have provided a steadily accumulating account of the reasons for non-take up. Various explanations have been proferred, involving a range of different factors. Most recently, research has demonstrated the importance of seeing take up as a complex decision process within which a series of interelated influences have an effect. This decision process, and the factors which influence it, have formed the central focus of this present study.

The evidence presented in this report is drawn from a research study carried out among a representative sample of eligible non-claimants in the London Borough of Hackney. The sample was identified from a household survey conducted to estimate the level of benefit take up within the Borough.[1] This earlier survey, which covered interviews with over 2,000 households, yielded a large pool of eligible non-claimants. On two counts, the availability of such a sample provided a valuable opportunity for take up research. First, it enabled the study to be prospective—much previous research has been confined to claimants' retrospective explanations of delays in claiming. Second it enabled more than one benefit to be covered since the previous study had included a range of means tested benefits. In this respect again it differs from previous research which has tended to concentrate on a single benefit.

Before embarking on a detailed account of the present study, it is necessary to describe the framework within which it was designed. A brief account of the benefits covered and the findings of earlier research on the take up of these benefits form a natural starting point.

1.2 The benefits

The three benefits covered by the study, supplementary benefit (SB), housing benefit (HB) and family income supplement (FIS) represented the only weekly paid means tested benefits available within the previous social security system.[2] All other income related benefits, of which there were a number, were awarded only when a special need or circumstance arose (eg free

---

(1) The Hackney Benefit Study was carried out by Jane Ritchie and Judith England at SCPR (Ritchie and England, 1988). It was undertaken on behalf of the London Borough of Hackney.

(2) The study was carried out prior to the introduction of the new social security scheme in April 1988 when supplementary benefit was replaced by income support and family income supplement by family credit.

prescriptions, fares to hospital, milk tokens etc). Of the three, supplementary benefit was perhaps the most important since it was the basic benefit available to those who were not in full time work and whose resources fell below a specified level. It was introduced in 1966 as successor to National Assistance, which itself was introduced in the 1940's as a small mopping up benefit for those ineligible for the new National Insurance benefits. However as insurance benefit levels were set below and have remained below those for national assistance and supplementary benefit a much larger segment of the population than was originally envisaged became eligible for the benefit. Subsequently, and with increasing levels of unemployment, it became an integral part of the income maintenance system. In 1986, there were 4.9 million claimants of whom over threequarters were either unemployed or pensioners. Expenditure on SB in 1986 was £7,509 millions.

The second benefit, housing benefit is payable, in respect of housing costs, to people with incomes below specified levels, irrespective of whether members of household are in employment. It was developed from three separate and distinct schemes: rent rebates, a system of help with rent for local authority tenants dating back to the 1930's; rent allowances, a similar scheme for private tenants, available since the 1950's; and rate rebates, for tenants and owner occupiers, introduced in the 1960's. These benefits were brought together as housing benefit in 1982. Prior to this time, the administration of housing rebates and allowances had been separately administered by the DHSS for supplementary benefit recipients and by local authorities for all other claimants. In 1982, the entire administration of housing benefit was transferred to local authorities. In 1986, around 7 million households were in receipt of housing benefit at a total cost of £4,459 millions.

Family income supplement was the smallest of the three benefits, both in cost and number of beneficiaries. It was available to families in employment, provided they were in full time work, either as wage earners or self employed people. Estimates for 1986 were that two hundred thousand families were in receipt of the benefit at a cost of £130 millions.

Ever since means tested benefits were introduced, there has always been a shortfall in the proportions of eligible people claiming their entitlement. The most recent official estimates show the following take up levels for the three benefits covered in this study.

	Take up rate	Number eligible not claiming	Annual total unclaimed
Supplementary benefit (1983)	76%	1,290,000	£570m
Housing benefit (1984)	77%	1,910,000	£500m
Family income supplement (1983–84)	54%	150,000	£57m

Source: DHSS, Social Security Statistics 1987

Note: The estimated take up rates given in the table are caseload based whereas the amounts unclaimed are expenditure based. Expenditure based estimates of take up (amount unclaimed as a proportion of total entitlement) are always higher than caseload based estimates because average amounts awarded tend to be higher than average unclaimed entitlements. Take up rates quoted in the literature are invariably caseload based.

There have been some changes in take up levels over the years and it is known that there are differential rates of take up among different claimant groups. There is also some debate about what the specific levels of take up are and how they should be estimated. However no estimate has ever put take-up of any means tested benefit (other than certificated housing benefit) much above 80% and the take-up of FIS has always been notably low.

1.3 A review of previous take up research

During the 1970's and early 1980's there was a steady flow of research on the take up of means tested benefits. Although the findings of the research still leave many questions unanswered, the picture of what prevents, or delays, people claiming is now becoming clearer. An important contribution to this understanding has come from the development of models or hierarchies to describe processes involved in a decision to claim. One particularly influential model was developed by Kerr to explain the decisions surrounding a claim for supplementary pension (Kerr, 1983). Drawing on previous research he developed six conceptually different reasons for claiming and suggested that these six main 'constructs' comprise a series of thresholds through which a person must pass before he or she makes a claim. The model assumes that all six thresholds must be crossed before a claim will be made. The thresholds are as follows:

1. Perceived need—the individual's perception of the extent to which he or she is having difficulty making ends meet;

2. Basic knowledge—the individual's awareness of the existence of the benefit;

3. Perceived eligibility—the individual's perception of the likelihood they are eligible for the benefit;

4. Perceived utility—the individual's perception of the utility of the benefit meeting his specific needs;

5. Beliefs and feeling about the application procedure—the sum of all the negative and positive forces exerted by an individual's beliefs about the application procedure and about how he or she feels about those beliefs;

6. Perceived stability of situation—the extent to which beliefs about the instability of the individual's situation prevents him from applying.

The Kerr model has been adapted by Corden to examine the process of claiming FIS and was found to provide a valuable analytic framework (Corden, 1983). It is generally regarded as having made a substantial contribution to the clarification of ideas about the barriers to claiming a means tested benefit.

A slightly different representation of the process was suggested by Ritchie and Matthews in their study of rent allowance take up (Ritchie and Matthews, 1982). They suggest that a key element in the decision to claim is one of 'trade off' including many different and opposing influences. Only if the positive influences outweigh the negative influences will a claim be made.

The factors involved in the 'trade off' cover some of the same constructs proposed by Kerr including perceived need, perceived eligibility and beliefs about the claiming process. Additionally they suggest that attitudes towards income support, and the people who receive it, are other influential factors. Unlike Kerr, however, they suggest that any one element of the trade off may outweigh the others and hence precipitate or inhibit a claim.

Although models of the kind outlined help to clarify the processes involved in claiming decisions, they do not necessarily identify ways in which claiming behaviour might be changed. To do so, it is necessary to understand the key factors which might bring movement (ie across thresholds, weight positive or negative forces etc) and hence influence a decision to claim. There is now a growing body of evidence about the range of factors which may be involved, a brief summary of which is given below.

Information

In early take up research, ignorance was seen as a crucial cause of non-take up. It was the reason given by many non-claimants when asked why they had delayed making, or had not made, a claim. Hence, it was believed that if people were provided with information, either about the existence of the benefit, criteria for entitlement, or their own eligibility, a major problem would be overcome. A number of studies have shown that this is not the case. While eligible non-claimants may explain their behaviour in terms of ignorance, they still fail to apply when provided with information. (Taylor-Gooby, 1976; McDonagh (nd); Walker (nd); Meacher, 1972; and Kerr, 1983). It has been suggested that this is because other factors, such as negative attitudes towards benefit support, will inhibit people's receipt and utilisation of the relevant information.

This evidence should not suggest that information is unimportant. Indeed several studies have shown that genuine misconceptions about eligibility criteria were the major deterrent to a claim for some people. Similarly, ignorance of the benefit system is still an important inhibitor for people whose first language is not English (Tarpey, 1984). It is evident, however, that while general information about benefits is necessary, it is certainly not sufficient, to ensure a claim.

Uncertainty about entitlement

Criteria for entitlement to means tested benefits are generally complex. Even where the basic eligibility criteria are relatively straightforward (as in the case of FIS), the specific conditions for entitlement, or the effects of special circumstances, require detailed regulations. Most take up research has shown that such complexities make it difficult for people to recognise their eligibility. This can have one of two effects. It may leave people with the misconception that they are *not* entitled; or it may create so much uncertainty that a fear of a refusal becomes heightened. Although uncertainty about entitlement is never a fully satisfactory explanation of non-claiming (ie further information can always be sought), it can evidently delay, or even inhibit, making a claim.

Difficulties with the claim process

Several studies have shown that difficulties with claim procedures can act as deterrents to making a claim. For example, the requirement to obtain and fill in a claim form has been recorded as one of the reasons for not applying in many take up studies. Similarly, having to go to benefit offices, waiting to be seen, providing confirmatory evidence, the general 'hassle', as it is often termed, can act as inhibitors to making a claim (see, for example Kerr, Corden). In some cases the deterrent arises after some difficulty has been experienced (eg finding difficulties with the form); in other cases it is a perception of the difficulties involved that causes the problem. Such perceptions may have come from other peoples accounts of the claiming process, from media reports, or simply from an impression of what claiming a benefit involves.

Previous experience of claiming

There is some evidence to suggest that a refusal of benefit, or a bad experience when claiming will deter people claiming in future (eg Corden). This can occur even if a different benefit is involved. A previous refusal can have one of two effects; it can make people more uncertain about their eligibility, even if their circumstances have changed; or it can increase the reluctance to ask in case they are turned down a second time. This reluctance arises because being turned down is seen as more than a simple administrative decision. It can carry connotations of fear about 'greed' or 'scrounging' since people may feel they have just asked for something to which they were not entitled (see Ritchie and Matthews). A previous bad experience of claiming can act as a deterrent simply to avoid being 'humiliated' or 'having to go through the hassle' a second time. People may be deterred by their own experiences or unfavourable accounts from friends or relations.

Social acceptability

A number of recent studies have shown that other people, whether in a formal or informal capacity, can have an important influence on the decision to claim (eg Kerr, Corden, Ritchie and Matthews). Friends, relatives or neighbours can be particularly effective in encouraging claims, especially if they themselves have claimed successfully in the past (Corden). Similarly, people in official positions, such as doctors, solicitors, advice workers, rent officers etc, can be influential in the decision process. Ritchie and Matthews suggest that the positive influence of other people may work directly, by enhancing the information network about the scheme; or indirectly, by providing the authority, legitimacy and acceptability to make a claim. A similar explanation is that the support of other people overcomes the view that 'ordinary people' do not claim benefits since they are for 'poor' or 'undeserving' groups (see, for example, Page and Weinberger). It is, of course, the case that the influence of other people can also work negatively in that they can reinforce attitudes or feelings already held.

The desirability of 'managing'

There is now considerable evidence to suggest that a perception of 'need' is crucial in the process of deciding to claim a benefit (see eg Kerr, Ritchie and Matthews). There is also some evidence, however, that people will avoid perceiving need because it is an admission of 'not managing'. Ritchie and Matthews have examined this issue in some detail and suggest that the relationship between 'managing' and 'need' is close. They argue that, below a certain subjective level of income, managing can be seen as one strategy to avoid reaching a state of need. The latter may only be reached in desperate circumstances. People can perceive themselves as managing, (which is acceptable) and not in need, (which is unacceptable) despite their proximity. Explanations can be found in people's expectations, in the existence of choice, and crucially in the importance of being independent. An admission of being unable to manage is an admission of not being able to support yourself and hence a failure to be independent. Independence appears to be at the end of many chains of questioning, a fundamental and unquestioned value in this society.

The role of the 'breadwinner'

A few studies have suggested that the role of the 'breadwinner' may be challenged by a claim for benefits, particularly when the 'budgeting' and 'providing' roles are quite separate. Taylor-Gooby suggested, for example, that women are sometimes reluctant to make their husbands pursue claims since it implies that the household income is insufficient. (Taylor-Gooby, 1974). Similarly, Ritchie and Matthews draw attention to the fact that women, because of their greater involvement in household budgeting, seemed keener than their husbands to find ways of supplementing the household income through benefits. There is evidence to suggest that some men find it difficult to admit that they cannot provide for their families' needs and hence, in some way, prevent the claim occurring.

Negative attitudes towards benefit support

In early take up research, 'stigma' was identified as a major explanatory factor in causes on non-take up. More recently, there has been some questioning of the concept. Allison, for example has suggested that stigma is of little consequence as a deterrent to claiming (Allison, 1982). Others have argued that stigma has simply become a residual category for all negative attitudes towards benefits (Kerr). It is certainly true that the term was over used and ill defined in much of the early research. More recent research, however, has attempted to clarify the concepts it represents. This has been helpful in two ways. First, it has begun to illuminate the complex mass of attitudes, beliefs and feelings which were formerly lumped together as stigma (see, for example, Corden, Ritchie and Matthews). Secondly, it has distinguished between the *feeling* of being stigmatised and the *process* of stigmatisation (Taylor-Gooby, 1976; Golding and Middleton, 1982). This has led researchers to conclude that the study of the origins of attitudes should 'move away from stigma as a state of mind attributed to the claimant or to his (sic) neighbours and towards the practices and procedures of official agencies'

(Briggs and Rees, 1980). In their recent review of benefit take up, Cohen and Tarpey suggest that such clarifications are a major step forward and add broader dimensions to the take up debate (Cohen and Tarpey, 1985).

1.4 The focus of the present study

The research evidence described above had provided considerably insight into the major causes of non-take up. Nevertheless, there were still some key questions left unanswered. First, would the Kerr threshold model have application to other benefits and other types of claimant groups. Second, what is the relative importance of factors which inhibit a decision to claim. And perhaps most important, what are the most powerful positive influences on a decision to claim.

It was with these questions in mind that the opportunity arose to undertake the present study among a sample of eligible non-claimants. Its focus was on two main lines of enquiry.

- an examination of the Kerr threshold model as an explanation of claiming behaviour.

- an examination of the role and importance of factors which positively or negatively influence the decision to claim.

The Kerr Threshold Model

As noted previously, the Kerr threshold model was originally developed and tested in a study of supplementary pension. It was also used, in modified form, by Corden in research concerning the take up of FIS. The present study provided an ideal opportunity to test the model across a range of benefits (ie SB, HB and FIS) and to examine its effectiveness for different claiming groups (ie pensioners, non-pensioners, one and two parent families, employed, unemployed etc).

Because the sample was derived from the Hackney Benefit Study, Kerr's design could not be followed exactly (see next chapter). However, where possible the procedures and the questions employed to measure respondents positions on the thresholds were kept the same.

The Competing Forces

The second main objective of the study was to examine the balance of forces which encourage or inhibit a claim and to identify their effect on claiming behaviour. To do this measures of the main influences thought to affect claiming behaviour were developed. These were used both to examine respondents' own explanations of their claiming behaviour and in an alternative approach to modelling which was developed during the course of the study. A full description of the design of the study and the sample on which it is based is given in the next chapter.

The study design

2.1 Hackney: an inner city area

The study described in the following pages was carried out in the London Borough of Hackney. This Borough is situated in the east of London, with a population of around 180,000 people. Like many other inner city areas, Hackney is characterised by many of the now well documented features of poor urban living. In his book about Hackney, Paul Harrison suggests that three closely related factors define the problems of such areas (Harrison, 1983). First, their industries are often declining, accompanied by a high level of unemployment. Secondly, they tend to be areas of particularly bad housing with a mixture of old Victorian terraces and more modern council housing, frequently of very poor design. Third, such areas have higher than average concentrations of manual, low skilled and unskilled workers, and of people dependent on the state for full or partial income support.

In Hackney, the level of poverty and disadvantage is high. The level of gross weekly earnings for all male full time workers averaged £167 in 1983, well below the level for Greater London as a whole (£200).[1] Fourteen per cent of all male full-time workers earned less than £100 per week, with 42% earning less than £150. The level of gross weekly earnings for all women in full-time employment follows a similar pattern with the average of £115 for Hackney again below the level of £131 for Greater London. Nineteen per cent of all women working full time earned less than £75 per week, while 35% earned less than £100.

Levels of earnings only reflect the circumstances of the working population. The last census showed that 16% of economically active men and 10% of economically active women were unemployed. For Greater London, these figures were 9% and 6% respectively. Hackney has the highest proportion of lone parents of any inner London Borough (15% compared to the second highest borough, Lambeth, with 14%), the second highest proportion of large families (8% of families have 3 or more children) and the second highest proportion of families with children under 5 (14%). Hackney also contains a high proportion of households headed by a person born in the New Commonwealth or Pakistan, 21% as opposed to 10% in Greater London.

The Hackney Benefit Study,[2] showed that in 1983, 45% of householders in Hackney received one or more means tested benefit. A further 15% of householders were identified as eligible for, although not receiving, an income related benefit and at least 3% more were well within scope. Thus in the early eighties, almost two out of every three households in the Borough were entitled to state support on the grounds of low income.

---

(1) New Earnings Survey 1983. The figures include overtime pay, bonus payments and shift allowances.
(2) Details of the Hackney Benefit Study are given in the following sections.

Paul Harrison suggests that the concentration of so many disadvantaged people in a single area produces other effects; local government poor in resources and sometimes in the quality of staffing; a poor health service, since doctors cannot find reasonable accommodation; a low level of educational attainment; higher levels of vandalism, crime and family breakdown; and, wherever divergent communities live together, conflicts based on religion or race. Harrison cautions, however, that such features are not confined to inner city areas: 'It is important not to consider the inner city as an isolated phenomena... They simply suffer from problems in a denser more visible form.'

The findings of this study relate only to Hackney. The extent to which they can be generalised to other inner city areas, or even less deprived areas, is debatable. On the one hand, the concentration of so many claimants in one area and the deprivation of the area itself is likely to have an effect on claiming behaviour. Alternatively, as Paul Harrison suggests, inner city areas have many features in common and none of these features are confined to such disadvantaged areas. Either way, it is important that the area context of the study is noted.

2.2 The sample of non-claimants

The sample for the present research was derived from the Hackney Benefit Study, which was carried out in the autumn of 1983. This study was undertaken to investigate the level of take up of means tested benefits within the Borough and to identify the characteristics of eligible non-claimants. The benefits covered by the study were housing benefit, supplementary benefit, family income supplement and free school meals.

The sample for the survey comprised 2,077 randomly selected households within which all claim units[1] (2,835) were identified. In all participating claim units a screen questionnaire was administered to assess potential eligibility for the benefits concerned. This assessment was made through a series of broad income checks. If the claim unit's income was at or below a specified level, and they were not already in receipt of the relevant benefit, they were taken through to a full assessment interview. The assessment interview then collected items of information from which a more comprehensive estimate of entitlement could be made. A total of 2,351 screen interviews (2,132 about householder claim units, 219 about non-householder claim units) and 560 full assessment interviews were carried out during the course of the study.

Of the 560 claim units that took part in the full assessment interview, 346 units were positively assessed as eligible for, but not receiving benefit.[2] These eligible non-claimants formed the main population of interest for the present follow up study. They were distributed across the three benefits as follows:

---

(1) A claim unit is defined as a single person or a married (or living as married) couple and their dependent children.
(2) The estimated take-up rates from the Hackney benefit study were HB 75%; SB 89%; FIS 42%; with the exception of SB they were thought to be compatible with national estimates for that time.

	Householder Claim Units	Non-Householder Claim Units	Total
Assessed as eligible for but not claiming			
HB	308	—	308
SB	59	15	74
FIS	24	1	25
Number eligible for one or more benefits	330	16	346

Sixty one claim units were assessed as eligible for more than one benefit. The main overlap occurred between housing benefit and either SB or FIS although there was a very small number of cases where the head of the claim unit was in part-time work, and where eligibility for both SB and FIS existed. Where eligibility for more than one benefit existed, a *main benefit* was assigned for the purpose of sample selection. Because of the smaller numbers of SB and FIS cases, these benefits were given priority over HB as the main benefit.

It was known at the time of the Hackney study that the number of eligible non-claimants for SB was an underestimate because claim units receiving housing benefit at the time were not assessed for eligibility for SB. It was estimated however that over 100 such claim units met basic SB eligibility criteria and were well in range of entitlement on income grounds.[1] It was decided to include claim units from this *'potentially eligible'* group in the follow-up study to compensate for the low numbers of SB cases. It needs to be noted, however, that this group received different treatment in the main study to those positively assessed as eligible (see next section).

The selection of the sample

The sample for the present study was selected from the two groups of eligible and potentially eligible non-claimants previously described. Before any selection could be made, certain cases had to be excluded from the sampling frames either because they did not wish to take part in any further interviews or because they had already been followed up for other reasons.[2] From the remaining cases, all claim units were included in the follow-up study, except in the case of those positively assessed as eligible for HB. Weighting (by a factor of two) has been applied in the analysis of the data to correct for this differential probability of selection. The resulting sample was composed as follows:

---

(1) This assessment was very approximate since only screen interview information was available for this group.
(2) Some in depth interviews with eligible non-claimants were undertaken as part of the Hackney Benefit Study. A separate study of one parent benefit was also undertaken with some of the eligible non-claimants, carried out by the Social Policy Research Unit at York University.

Main Sample	Positively assessed as eligible for	HB	Selected Sample 152	
		SB	55	222
		FIS	15	
Supplementary Sample	Potentially eligible for SB		113	
	Total selected sample[1]		335	

The two samples will be referred to hereafter as the 'main' sample and the 'supplementary' sample.

2.3 The four stages of the study

The present study describes the progress towards claiming of a group of eligible non-claimants over a period of almost two years. During this period, the four critical stages of the study were as follows:

Stage 1. Autumn 1983. Initial interviews for Hackney Benefit Study

- As has already been noted, all the claim units involved took part in an interview in the main Hackney study. The 222 cases in the main sample took part in *full assessment* interviews which lasted around 45–50 minutes. This covered numerous items necessary for benefit assessment, particularly relating to financial circumstances, as well as some general questions on attitudes towards claiming. The 113 claim units in the supplementary sample took part only in a *screen interview*, which was much shorter. This asked for less detailed information about personal circumstances, income, and benefits currently received.

Stage 2. May 1984 Information about entitlement

- Following the benefit assessments from the questionnaire data, all those who were positively assessed as eligible were sent a letter about their entitlement. This letter informed them of which benefit(s) they might be eligible for and advised them to make a claim (see copy in Appendix III). The letter was sent only to those in the main sample.

Stage 3. Summer 1984 The follow up interview

- The follow up interviews for this study were conducted in July and August 1984, approximately 2–3 months after letters were sent out. Of the 335 claim units approached 273 were found to be in scope for the study and 184 (ie 67% of 273) were interviewed. Sixty two claim units were found to be out of scope, either because they had moved out of the study area (28), could not be traced (6), or were found to have been claiming the benefit since before their first interview (28) (ie they were ineligible for follow up although the answers given on the first interview suggested otherwise). The sample of people interviewed comprised 97 eligible for HB, 77 eligible for SB and 10 eligible for FIS. A full

---

(1) These figures include the sample for the pilot study from which interviews were included in the final analysis.

account of the response rate, by type of benefit and sample type, is given in Appendix I.

The purpose of the follow up interviews was to establish whether a claim for benefit had been made since the first interview; whether they had thought about claiming or made any enquiries; whether they had undergone any change of circumstances which might have affected their eligibility; and to obtain an explanation of claiming or non-claiming behaviours.

Stage 4. July 1985 The record check at benefit offices

- At the time of the follow up interview, respondents were asked if the research team, at a later date, could approach selected benefit offices, to see if a claim had been made, and if so, whether it had been successful. The majority (80%) agreed and gave their written permission (see Appendix III). The record check was undertaken approximately one year after the follow up interviews at the following agencies; local Social Security Offices for SB; Hackney Housing Benefit Office for HB; and the FIS Unit at DHSS North Fylde Central Office (Blackpool) for Family Income Supplement.

The stages involved for the two sample groups are summarised in chart 2.1.

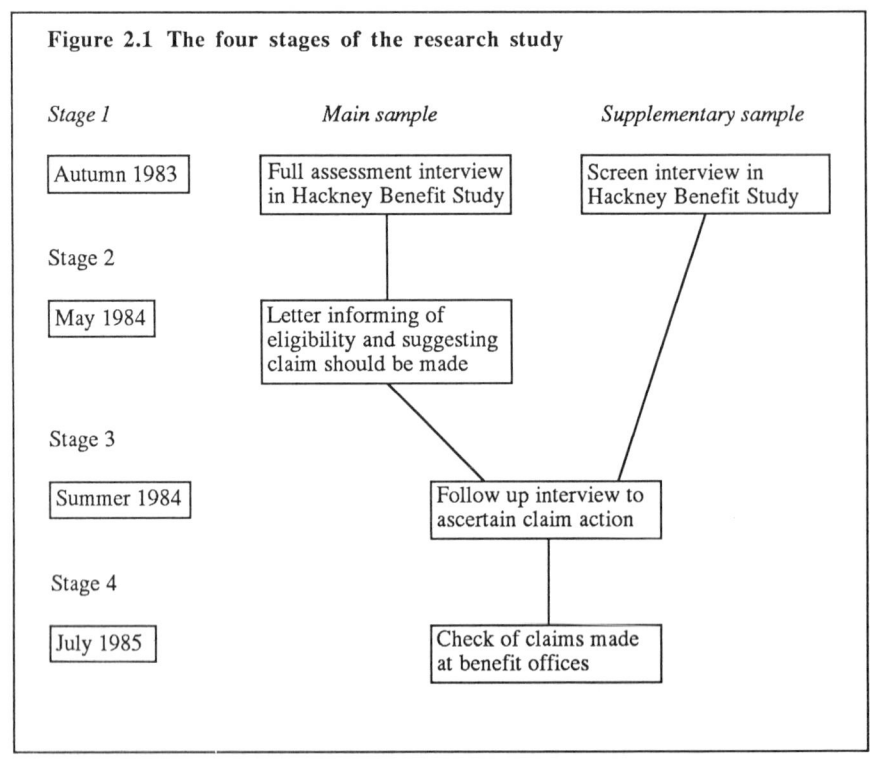

Figure 2.1 The four stages of the research study

Stage	Date	Main sample	Supplementary sample
Stage 1	Autumn 1983	Full assessment interview in Hackney Benefit Study	Screen interview in Hackney Benefit Study
Stage 2	May 1984	Letter informing of eligibility and suggesting claim should be made	
Stage 3	Summer 1984	Follow up interview to ascertain claim action	
Stage 4	July 1985	Check of claims made at benefit offices	

It is clear that participation in the study could well have had an effect on claiming behaviour, particularly for those in the main sample. The first interview would almost certainly have made them more aware of their potential entitlement to benefits and they then subsequently received a letter to this effect. The impact for those who took part only in the screen interview would certainly be less, although even so, their awareness of the benefits available could well have been increased.

As would be expected, the findings of the study show that people made claims throughout the period covered by the research. Despite this, more than half of the follow up sample had still not made a claim by July 1985, almost 2 years after the first interviews took place. It is the aim of this report to explain why this group of non-claimants still remained at the end of the study.

2.4 A profile of the eligible non-claimants

The characteristics of the sample interviewed (Summer 1984)

All the people interviewed in the follow up study had been assessed as in range of eligibility for a means tested benefit they were not claiming. For this reason they represent a very particular population which, when compared with the general population, inevitably contains disproportionate numbers of certain groups. Their profile, however, is complicated by the fact that two different sets of characteristics are operating. Although, in the first instance, they represent groups that are eligible for means tested benefit (eg low income, non-economically active), this distribution is affected by differential levels of take up within certain claimant groups (eg pensioners, one parent families). The resulting profile therefore represents the interactive effect of eligibility and non-claiming.

An example will help to clarify this point. The Hackney Benefit Study showed that around 90% of lone parent families were eligible for one or more means tested benefits. Thus, in any profile of eligible groups, lone parents would be expected to have a high representation. However, the study also showed that lone parents had a relatively high take up rate when compared with other groups. As a result of this counteractive effect, lone parents appear in relatively *small* proportions in the population of *eligible non-claimants*.

Table 2.1 shows the composition of the claim units interviewed in the follow up study. It is compared here with the profile of all claim units (whether eligible or not, claiming or not) identified in the Hackney Benefit Study. This shows two important features of the sample. First, it contains a high proportion of pensioners. This is because pensioners feature prominantly both in the population eligible for benefits *and* in the population of non-claimants. Secondly, the sample contains a very small proportion of non-householder claim units (and consequently a disproportionately low number of young single people).[1] This is partly because there is a smaller proportion of eligible non-claimants among non-householders than among householders but also because of greater non-response among non-householders.

---

(1) The Hackney Benefit Study showed that 87% of non-householder units in Hackney consisted of single people under pensionable age, the majority of whom were young adults.

Table 2.1 Composition of claim units interviewed in follow-up study (Summer 1984): Comparison with all claim units in Hackney (Autumn 1983)

Type of claim unit	Sample type Main sample	Sample type Supplementary sample	Total follow up sample	All claim units Hackney Benefit Study Autumn 1983
	%	%	%	%
Non-Pensioners				
Single person	26	12	24	42
Married couple	16	4	14	13
Lone parent with dependent children	4	2	4	8
Married couple with dependent children	25	4	21	16
Pensioners				
Single person	15	53	22	13
Married couple	14	24	16	8
With dependent children	—	—	—	*
Type of Claim Unit				
Householder unit	99	98	98	76
Non-householder unit	1	2	2	24
Total %	100	100	100	100
Base: All claim units:				
weighted	233	48	282	2,950
unweighted	135	49	184	2,835

Table 2.2 Composition of claim units by main benefit for which eligible

Composition of claim unit	Main Benefit HB	Main Benefit SB	Main Benefit FIS	Total sample
	%	%	No.	
Non-Pensioners				
Single person	22	28	—	24
Married couple	18	5	—	14
Lone parent with dependent children	4	2	(3)	4
Married couple with dependent children	24	9	(6)	21
Pensioners				
Single person	17	35	—	22
Married couple	15	20	—	16
Total %	100	100	—	100
Base: All claim units:				
weighted	192	81	9	282
unweighted	97	77	10	184

The composition of claim units varied considerably between the three benefit groups. Over half of the eligible non-claimants for supplementary benefit were pensioners compared with a third of the housing benefit non-claimants. Again this reflects the take up patterns identified in the Hackney

Benefit Study. Take up of housing benefit was found to be lower amongst eligible non-pensioners than amongst eligible pensioners. For supplementary benefit, the reverse was true, that is take up was higher amongst non-pensioners than amongst pensioners.

Table 2.3 shows other characteristics of the householder claim units interviewed, compared with the profile of all claim units identified in the Hackney Benefit Study. As noted previously, the sample contains a comparatively high proportion of older, retired people. A perhaps more notable feature of the distributions is the fact that the proportion in full time employment is very similar to that for the population in Hackney as a whole. Although people in full time work can claim means tested benefits (HB and FIS) their higher income levels are more likely to make them ineligible than groups in part time employment or those not working. The Hackney Benefit Study showed for example that 30% of people in full time employment were eligible for a means tested benefit compared with 73% in part time employment and 88% of those unemployed or not working for other reasons. However, it was also found that those working full time, who were eligible for benefits, had lower take up rates than other groups. This explains why they are represented in such sizeable proportions in the sample of eligible non-claimants. The same factors apply to owner occupiers who form 10% of the follow-up sample.

The evidence above shows how the sample interviewed compares with the general population. This is important as a base for interpreting the substantive findings which follow. It is also important however, to consider how well the sample represents the population of eligible non-claimants from which it is drawn. The comparisons which have been made show that the follow-up sample is deficient in non-householder claim units and hence under-represents young single people. This is because of a slightly higher level of attrition among non-householder claim units than among those headed by a householder. The householder sample, however, shows a fair representation of its parent population in terms of claim unit type, age, tenure and economic activity status.

Before continuing further, we must note the limitations placed on the analysis by the small size of certain groups. Two are of particular importance. First, we are unable to draw any conclusions about the FIS sample since it contains only 10 people. We have however shown the raw numbers in most of the tables and have always included them in the figures for the total sample. Second, the number of people in the sample from each of the ethnic minority groups is very small indeed (see table 2.3). This means we are prohibited from presenting any analysis by ethnic origin. This is particularly sad since the Hackney population contains a relatively high proportion of ethnic minority households. Unfortunately, however, none of the group is represented in sufficient size within the sample of eligible non-claimants.

Changes of circumstance since the first interview

The previous section described the composition and characteristics of the claim units when they were interviewed for the follow up study. In the nine months that had elapsed since the first interview, some of the claim units had experienced important changes in their circumstances.

Table 2.3 Characteristics of householder claim units interviewed in follow up study (Summer 1984): Comparison with all householder claim units in Hackney (Autumn 1983)

Demographic characteristics	Follow up sample	All householder claim units: Hackney Benefit Study (Autumn 1983)
Age of head of claim unit	%	%
Under 25	6	13
25–39	25	31
40–49	11	14
50—pensionable age	24	19
Pensionable age—69	16	8
70 or over	18	15
Economic activity status		
Full time employment	40	44
Part time employment	6	5
Unemployed	12	15
Wholly retired	34	20
Full time education	2	4
Other not working	7	12
Tenure		
Owner occupier	10	16
Tenant		
—local authority	63	55
—housing association	8	8
—private	18	20
—other or not known	1	2
Ethnic group		
West Indian or Guyanese	7	13
Indian, Pakistani, Bengali	2	2
African	3	3
Greek Cypriot	1	1
Turkish Cypriot	2	2
Other—non European	3	3
European—no group stated	82	74
Not given	*	2
Total %	100	100
Base: Householder claim units:		
weighted	276	2,238
unweighted	179	2,132

In summary, these were as follows:

Changes in: Composition of claim unit:

—gained dependent child	2%	⎫
—lost dependent child	2%	⎪
(eg left school, left home etc)		⎬ 11%
—became part of a couple	4%	⎪
—became single (ie separated or widowed)	3%	⎭

Pensionable status

—became of pensionable age	2%

Employment status

—became employed	8%	⎫
—changed number of hours worked	1%	⎪
(eg full or part time)		⎬ 17%
—became unemployed	4%	⎪
—retired	3%	⎪
—given up work for other reasons	1%	⎭

Accommodation

—moved house	2%

Clearly, some of the changes described above had an important effect on eligibility for benefits. Some of the claim units became ineligible for any means tested benefit, some became eligible for a different benefit, while others increased their level of entitlement. The implications of such changes are considered in detail in the next chapter.

Changes in claiming behaviour

3.1 Introduction

A period of nine months elapsed after the first interview (in which eligibility was assessed) and before the follow-up interview was undertaken. During this period the majority of participants in the study received a letter advising them to make a claim. After nine months the situation was as follows:

<blockquote>
Became CLAIMANT   35%
Still NON-CLAIMANT   65%
</blockquote>

One year later, when the record check at benefit offices was made, a further 9% were known to have become claimants. By this time, of course, all the respondents had taken part in the second interview which implicitly, if not explicitly, informed them of their potential eligibility. Despite this, and almost two years after the initial assessment was made, over half (56%) were still non-claimants.

Figure 3.1 *Claiming patterns over periods of study*

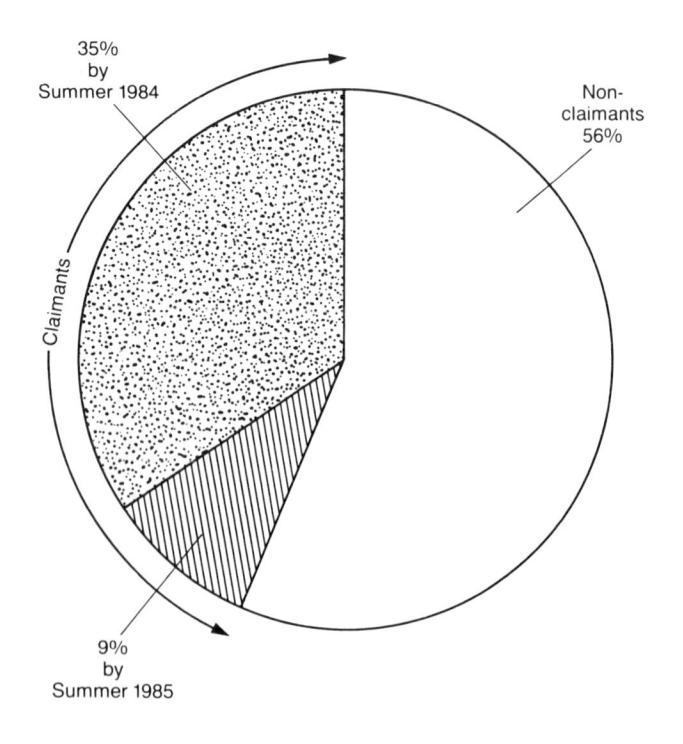

These findings are consistent with the results of previous research. Taylor-Gooby, for example, found that two-thirds of the eligible non-claimants of rent rebate who blamed ignorance for not claiming, still failed to claim after being given explicit information and advice about it (Taylor-Gooby 1976). Similar findings have been reported by Meacher (1972), McDonagh, and Walker. In the majority of cases, a failure to claim is not explained by an absence of knowledge about potential entitlement to the benefit.

It is the aim of this report to examine the factors that do inhibit claims. In order to do this, we shall be making an important divide between those who did make a claim after the Hackney Benefit Study interview and those who remained non-claimants. In this chapter, the characteristics and circumstances of the two groups are examined.

3.2 Changes after nine months

By the time of the follow up interview, just over one third of the sample had become claimants and the remaining two thirds were still non-claimants. The non-claimants, however, had not been entirely passive about claiming—some had taken action towards a claim and others had given it some serious thought. This left just over a third who, apparently, had given no thought to claiming at all.

Figure 3.2 *Claiming action after 9 months*

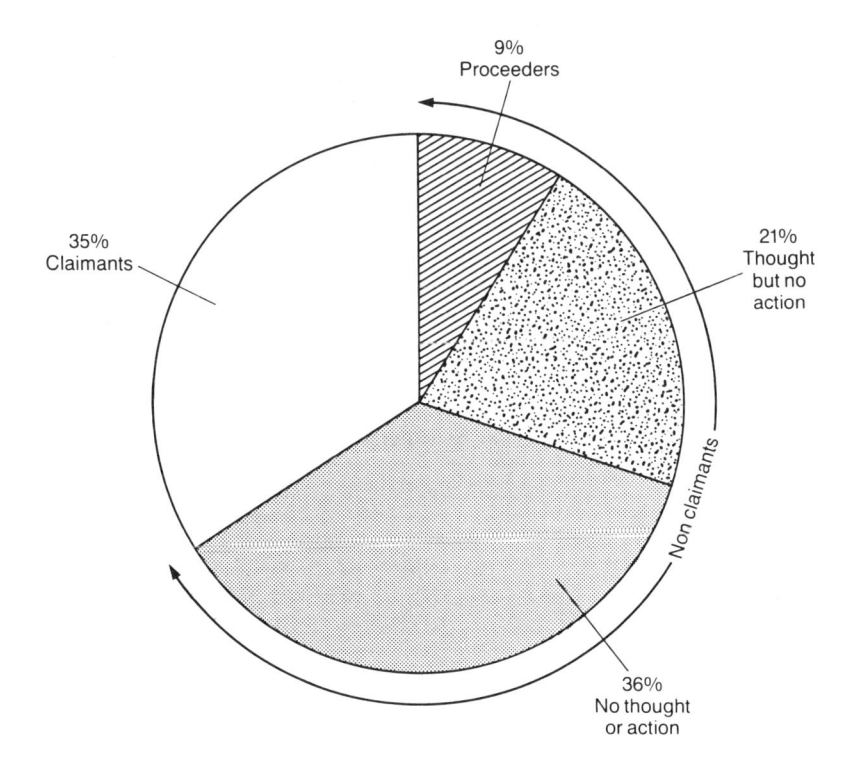

The Claimants

The majority of the claims were made in the six months following the first interview and *before* the letter informing about entitlement was sent. This pattern was much the same for the two sample groups as is shown below.

Table 3.1 Timing of claim, by sample type

Date of (first)* claim		Main Sample %	Supplementary Sample %	Total %
1st Interview	1983 September/October	7	2	6
	November/December	9	7	8
	1984 January/February	6	7	5
	March/April	6	4	7
Letter—Main sample only—	May	1	—	*
	June/July	4	4	4
	Not given/could not remember	4	4	4
No claim before 2nd interview		63	73	65
Total %		100	100	100
Base: All claim units				
weighted		234	48	282
unweighted		135	49	184

* A small proportion (5%) had made a second claim for benefit during the nine month interval.

Of those who knew the outcome of their claim, around 86% had been successful and 14% had been told they were ineligible. The picture across the different benefit groups was similar although a slightly higher proportion of the supplementary sample had been found ineligible (table 3.2). Of those who had been turned down, all but one remembered being given an explanation although none of them felt satisfied with what they had been told.

This group of claimants are of particular interest to this study since they had changed from being eligible non-claimants. The factors that stimulated them to make a claim are examined in the second part of the report. It may be useful here, however, to give some flavour of the various forces that were at work.

Table 3.2 Outcome of (first) claim by benefit group and sample type

Outcome of claim	HB	FIS	SB	Main Sample	Supplementary Sample	Total
	%	No.	%	%	No.	%
Awarded the benefit	67	(3)	90	72	10	73
Claim turned down	11	(1)	10	10	(3)	11
Not yet heard	21	(1)	—	18	(—)	16
Total %	100	—	100	100	—	100
Base: Claimants by Summer '84						
weighted	68	4	26	85	13	98
unweighted	32	5	27	50	14	64

Ms Lenton[1] is 32 and lives with her partner aged 25. She is employed on a freelance basis and therefore has an irregular pattern of income. She had vaguely thought about apply for housing benefit before but decided against it because 'it's so difficult for me, my income can be nil and then a couple of hundred by the nature of my work. There isn't a mean I can give.' Added to this, she was unhappy about the possibility of having to give detailed information about her living arrangements 'I think its none of their business and that's one of the reasons that stops me claiming things.' She was however led to a claim by the arrival of a large rates bill at a time when they were both short of money. 'The enormous amount of the rates—I'd never expected as much as that... I was out of work, Harry (partner) was on low money and the bill was very high and unfair.'

Mr. Gregory is 44 and lives with his wife and three sons (aged 7, 6 and 4). He is a civil servant, on a fairly low income, and owns his house which is in an action area. In the course of applying for an improvement grant he discovered that he would get a 90% grant (rather than 75%) if he was receiving a rate rebate or FIS. This together with the rising level of the rates—they 'have been going up every year about £100', led him to claim a rebate. He had not done so before for two reasons. First, he was very uncertain about his eligibility because he is a 'civil servant'. Perhaps more important, he was not at all keen to give the name of his employer as part of his application 'I felt this application has to be proceessed not only by my employer but by a personal secretary who will come to know my financial situation and we are working together in the same office.'

The proceeders

People were defined as proceeders (9%) if they had taken some action towards a claim. For the majority, the action involved obtaining a claim form, although just under half had also made enquiries at the appropriate benefit office. Only a few, however, had got as far as completing the claim form but none of them actually submitted the claim. In one or two cases, the reasons for this were connected with the form itself, either because they did not want to give the kind of information that was required, or because they found the form difficult to complete. More commonly, however, the process of claiming got halted at this point for quite different reasons. These included:

A preference to 'manage'
'I thought that when my wife packs up work will be the time to fill it in. We can manage to pay the rent with our present income'.

Uncertainty about eligibility
'We didn't think we would be entitled to it... the amount of money we earn we thought we wouldn't qualify.'

Negative feelings about being in receipt of benefit
'My husband got it—I told him not to fill it in... we don't grab anything that's going. ...we can hold our head up high.'

Change of circumstance
'My husband got an interview for a job by the time we'd filled the form in so we didn't post it.'

---

(1) This and all following 'names' are fictitious.

Previous experiences of claiming
'In the past I claimed HB and I was overpaid and there have been a lot of problems in consequence of this'.

The 'thinkers'

A further quarter of the sample said they had given some thought to a claim since the first interview. Of these, around half had given the matter some careful consideration while the rest said they had not really thought about it very seriously. The majority had thought about claiming before Christmas 1983—in some cases stimulated by the first interview. This, of course, was before the main sample received the letter informing them of their entitlement.

Illustration of the conflicting pressures in the minds of people who had thought seriously, but not yet taken any action towards a claim, is provided in the following example of a family eligible for housing benefit.

Both partners were in work, the husband in full time employment and the wife in part time work. They had been sent a letter by SCPR, and had been 'very pleased' about their potential eligibility. The event that had made them give serious thought to a claim, as in an earlier example, was the arrival of a rates bill. 'It was when the rates bill arrived for £600. We did not know where the money would come from... Without extra help we cannot go on living as we are.' When asked if anything had put them off the idea of claiming, the wife (who was interviewed) answered, 'Just the idea of filling in a form, and then at the end you are refused' And about going to the local office: 'There might be other women there who are unemployed and they would think, what the hell is she doing here?' Despite feeling hard up and being worried about how to pay the rate bill, the family had delayed claiming because of anxieties about the claiming process itself.

The claim resistors

The final group appear to be most resistant to the idea of a benefit claim. Despite an interview, and for many, a letter informing of their eligibility, they had apparently not considered the idea of claiming at all. This group forms just over a third of all participants in the follow up study.

The reasons for resisting a claim are numerous and will be discussed in detail in the next part of the report. The two illustrative cases below raise some of the issued involved.

> Mr George is 38 and unemployed; his wife works part time. From the evidence they gave it seemed that they were entitled to supplementary benefit and received a letter to this effect. They had, however, completely dismissed the idea of claiming 'It's very borderline so it's not worth the bother. I had social security money about 15 years ago and I don't want to bother with it. It was so much degradation. You queue for hours and hours. They treat you as 4th class citizens. Unless I was really hard up, I wouldn't even consider it.'

> Mr Bradford (42) lives with his wife and four children (aged between 10 and 16). He works full time and is eligible for FIS. He has not however, thought about making a claim, despite having received a letter about his entitlement. Essentially he feels that they have managed without it while their children have been growing

up and there now seems little point 'I don't want to go to all the trouble... All these years we've survived without it—now soon my daughter will be going out to work. If we were going to do it we'd have done it years ago when they were babies.

Differences in extent of action taken

Table 3.3 shows how the four groups previously described distribute in relation to benefit group and sample type. As can be seen the proportion of claimants was very similar for the three main benefits. There was, however, a difference in claiming activities between the two sample groups. Those who had been positively assessed as eligible and who had received a letter to this effect were more likely to have claimed, or to have given the matter some thought, than those in the supplementary sample. Although it is tempting to think that this was a direct result of receiving the letter about eligibility, we have already seen that most of the claims had been made *before* the letter arrived. The difference between the two sample groups is the result of a number of factors that will be unravelled in the course of the following chapters.

Table 3.3 Extent of claim action taken, by benefit group and sample type

	HB	SB	FIS	Main sample	Supplementary sample	Total sample
	%	%	No.	%	%	%
Claimant	35	33	(4)	37	27	35
Non-claimant	65	67	(5)	63	73	65
—taken action	11	4	—	10	2	8
—thought about claim	26	11	—	22	12	21
—no thought	28	52	(5)	31	59	36
Base: All claim units						
weighted	192	81	9	233	49	282
unweighted	97	77	10	135	49	184

Figure 3.3 shows that there are very marked differences in patterns of claiming among different age groups. In general, it was the youngest age groups that showed the highest claiming rates. Although the numbers are too small to draw any firm conclusions, it would appear that those who had fairly recently become pensioners (ie aged 60/65 to 70) showed a slightly higher propensity to claim, or at least to think about a claim, than the age groups on either side of them.

In addition to age, certain other characteristics appear to be associated with a resistance to have claimed the benefit concerned (table 3.4.). Although, again, some caution is needed because of the small base sizes, there is some evidence to suggest that married couples with dependent children show a slightly lower propensity to have claimed when compared with other married couples or with lone parent families. Owner occupiers also show lower claiming rates and comparatively high proportions who have

Figure 3.3 *Claim action among different age groups*

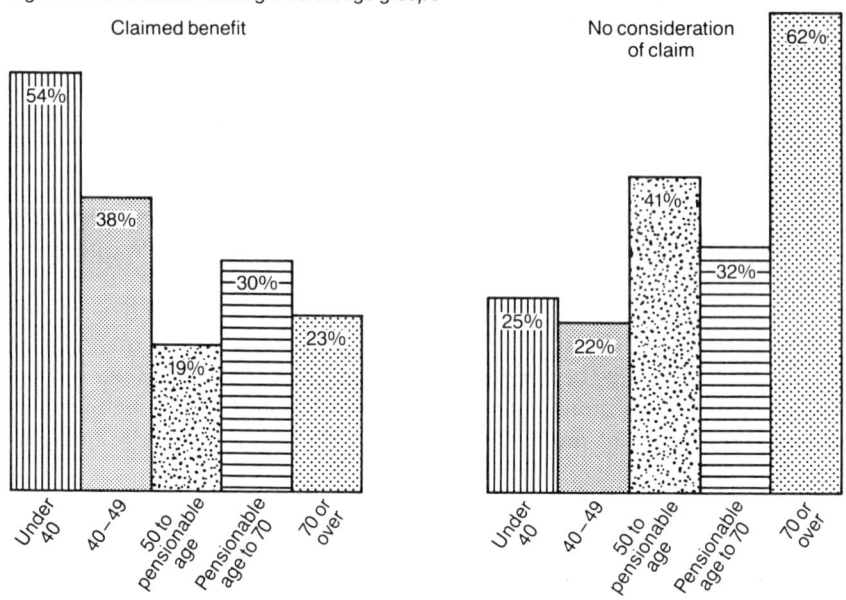

Claimed benefit:
- Under 40: 54%
- 40-49: 38%
- 50 to pensionable age: 19%
- Pensionable age to 70: 30%
- 70 or over: 23%

No consideration of claim:
- Under 40: 25%
- 40-49: 22%
- 50 to pensionable age: 41%
- Pensionable age to 70: 32%
- 70 or over: 62%

Table 3.4 Claiming action by composition and circumstances of claim unit

Characteristics of claim units	CLAIMED benefit	NOT CLAIMED but taken action or thought	NOT CLAIMED and no thought	Total %	Base (weighted)
Composition of claim unit Non-pensioners					
Single person	%	38	34	29	100	66
Married couple	%	52	17	31	100	39
Lone parent with dep. children	No.	(5)	(5)	(2)	—	11
Married couple with dep. children	%	37	33	32	100	60
Pensioners					
Single parent	%	24	25	50	100	61
Married couple	%	26	32	41	100	45
Economic activity status					
Full time employment	%	25	39	35	100	112
Part time employment	No.	(8)	(5)	(4)	—	16
Unemployed	%	82	8	10	100	38
Wholly retired	%	27	36	49	100	94
Other not working	%	32	32	4	100	22
Tenant					
Owner occupier	%	26	33	41	100	27
Tenant—local authority	%	35	28	37	100	173
—housing association	%	40	30	30	100	23
—private	%	37	27	35	100	51
—other or not known	No.	—	(2)	—	—	2

given the matter no thought when compared with other tenure groups. Amongst those who were not retired, people who were in full time employment show generally lower claiming rates than other groups, and particularly when compared with the unemployed. (It should be noted that recipients of unemployment benefit normally move onto supplementary benefit when their entitlement to UB ceases (after twelve months) and this will in part explain their high level of claiming.)

Changes after two years

Before we move on to consider what further claims there had been after the follow up interview, it is important to note the changes in the eligibility status of some of the non-claimants. As we described in the previous chapter a number of the non-claimants had experienced changes in their circumstances and in some cases these had made them ineligible for the benefit concerned on basic eligibility criteria (eg a person previously assessed as eligible for SB had obtained full time work). In addition, there were also some cases where there had apparently been changes in income which brought their resources above the required level for entitlement[1].

As a consequence of these changes we identified a total of 5% of cases where the non-claimant appeared to have become ineligible on basic eligibility criteria and a further 5% whose income brought them above the required level for entitlement. The incidence of these cases was higher among the SB sample as is shown below:

	HB	SB	FIS	TOTAL
Ineligible on basic criteria	—	10%	—	5%
'Ineligible' on income grounds	5%	2%	(1)	5%
Total 'ineligible'	5%	12%	(1)	10%
Base: Total follow up sample (weighted)	192	81	9	282

For most of the analysis, we decided to leave these cases in the sample. There are three reasons for this. First, as far as the income level is concerned there is inevitably some uncertainty surrounding our benefit assessment since they were undertaken from survey data. Perhaps more important, the non-claimants could not themselves be sure of the outcome of a claim since their income was very close to the margins where they would be entitled. The second group, who had become ineligible through no longer meeting basic eligibility criteria have been left in partly because they had remained non-claimants while they were eligible (ie prior to the follow up interview) and could well become eligible again. It is also the case that many of this group could well have become eligible for one of the other benefits (ie SB non-claimant becoming eligible for HB or FIS when they take up full time employment). Since they were only interviewed about one benefit (ie the main benefit) we could incorporate this change within the analysis. Nevertheless,

---

(1) These cases were identified through applying an uprated version of the benefit assessment programmes used for the Hackney Benefit Study.

given the proximity of all these doubtful cases to eligibility for means tested benefits, we have no reservations about continuing to include them in most of the analysis.

3.3 Changes after two years

It was noted at the start of this chapter that 9% of the sample made a claim between July 1984 (when the follow up study took place) and July 1985 when the record checks at benefit offices were undertaken. It is possible to view this group as late or reluctant claimants since it had taken them some time to make the decision to claim. Although we have no information about what eventually triggered the claim, it is possible to say something about their circumstances and characteristics, as described in the July 1984 interview.

It should be noted that the number of claims made after the follow up interview were proportionately the same for the three benefits. In fact by the end of the study's monitoring, exactly the same proportion (43%) of the HB and SB groups had made a claim (table 3.5). Although there was a relatively larger increase amongst the supplementary sample than among the main sample, it has to be remembered that the former group had not received as much stimulus to claim (ie they had not had a letter) prior to the follow up interview.

Table 3.5 Claiming action by benefit group and sample type

Claiming action	HB	SB	FIS	Main sample	Supplementary sample	Total
	%	%	No.	%	%	%
Claimed between						
—Autumn '83 and Summer '84	35	33	(4)	37	27	35
—Summer '84 and Summer '85	8	10	(1)	8	12	9
Still non-claimant at end of study	57	57	(4)	55	61	57
Total %	100	100	—	100	100	100
Base: All claim units						
weighted	192	81	9	233	49	282
unweighted	97	77	10	135	49	184

To examine the characteristics of those who made a claim after the follow up interview, it is useful to bear in mind the characteristics of the earlier claimants described in the previous section. This provides the opportunity to see if any new groups are emerging as late claimers or whether the same groups remain resistant. Figure 3.4 shows a profile of the people who claimed, analysed by the composition of the claim unit. Although there were some new claimants from all of the claim unit types, it can be seen that the relative profile has remained much the same. The same picture emerges when other characteristics are examined (see figure 3.5). We can see for example that the group who just reached pensionable age have shown a greater increase in claims than the age groups on either side. Similarly, those in full time employment and owner occupiers, two groups which were previously noted as 'resistors' to claiming have not greatly changed their position.

Figure 3.4 *Claiming action by composition of claim unit*

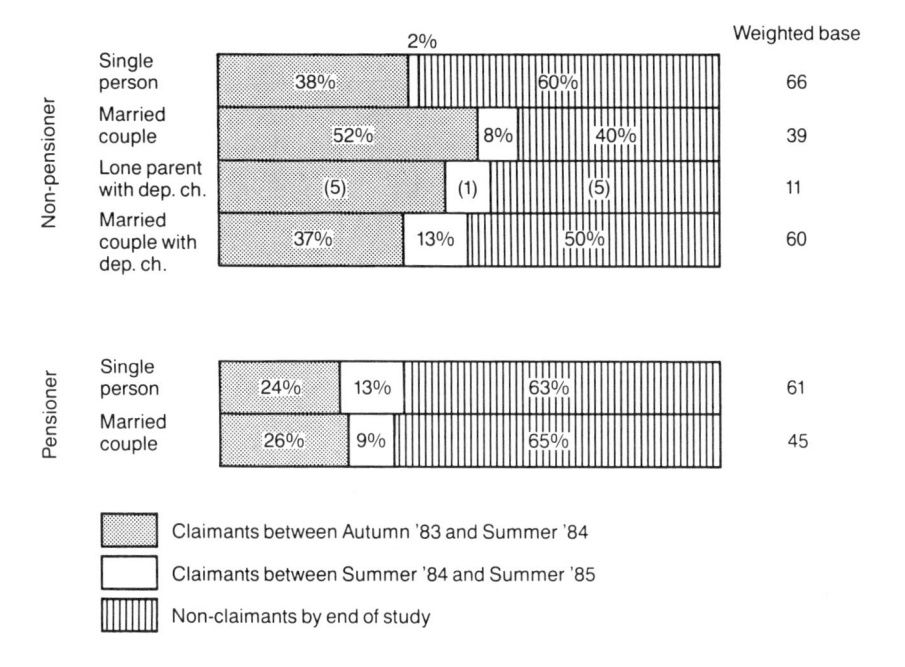

		Autumn '83–Summer '84	Summer '84–Summer '85	Non-claimants	Weighted base
Non-pensioner	Single person	38%	2%	60%	66
	Married couple	52%	8%	40%	39
	Lone parent with dep. ch.	(5)	(1)	(5)	11
	Married couple with dep. ch.	37%	13%	50%	60
Pensioner	Single person	24%	13%	63%	61
	Married couple	26%	9%	65%	45

▨ Claimants between Autumn '83 and Summer '84
☐ Claimants between Summer '84 and Summer '85
▥ Non-claimants by end of study

The evidence so far suggests that four groups might be identified as being 'claim resistors'. These are

- people approaching or well over pensionable age
- two parent families
- owner occupiers
- people in full time employment.

All these groups had in fact been identified in the Hackney Benefit Study as target populations for increasing take up. It seems, therefore, that not only do they have disproportionately low take up rates, they continue to be the most resistant to claiming even amongst a population of similarly eligible non-claimants.

There are two ways in which these figures can be viewed. On the one hand we can conclude that groups who display low take up rates are likely to remain resistant to claiming. A rather more positive view, however, would be to say that even among the resistant groups there are people who will change from non-claimants to claimants because of some stimulus to claim. We shall be examining what makes these groups resistant and what eventually precipitates a claim in the following sections.

Before leaving these 'late' claimants it is of interest to consider how much thought they had given to claiming before the follow up interview. It might be expected, for example, that it would be those who had previously taken some action (ie the 'proceeders') or those who had given the matter serious thought, who would be most likely to claim. Although there is a slight indication of such a relationship, we still find that 10% of those who said they

Figure 3.5 *Claim action by characteristics of head of claim unit*

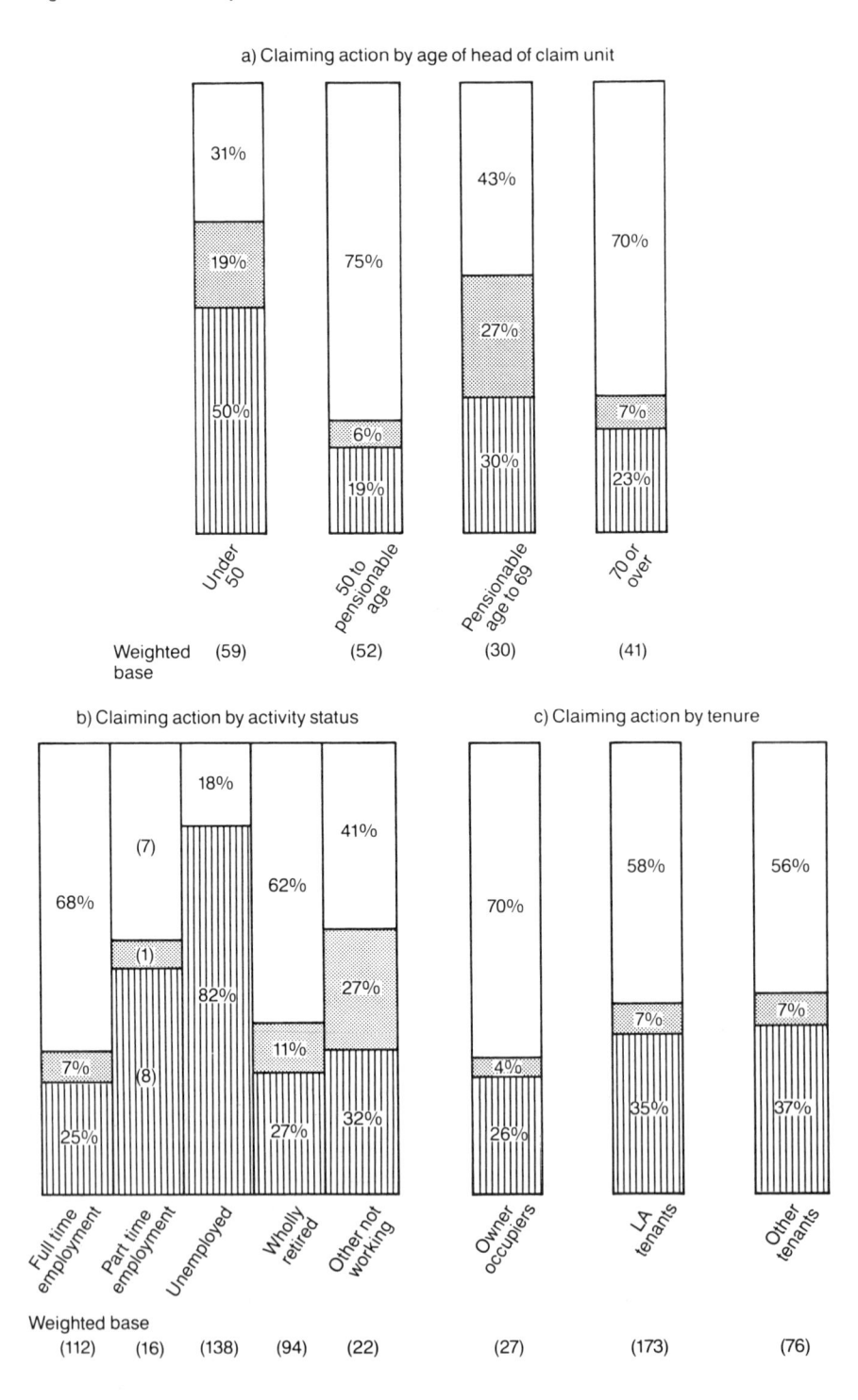

a) Claiming action by age of head of claim unit

	Under 50	50 to pensionable age	Pensionable age to 69	70 or over
Top	31%	75%	43%	70%
Middle	19%	6%	27%	7%
Bottom (split)	50%	19%	30%	23%
Weighted base	(59)	(52)	(30)	(41)

b) Claiming action by activity status

	Full time employment	Part time employment	Unemployed	Wholly retired	Other not working
Top	68%	(7)	18%	62%	41%
Upper mid	—	(1)	—	—	27%
Mid	7%	(8)	82%	11%	—
Bottom	25%	—	—	27%	32%
Weighted base	(112)	(16)	(138)	(94)	(22)

c) Claiming action by tenure

	Owner occupiers	LA tenants	Other tenants
Top	70%	58%	56%
Middle	4%	7%	7%
Bottom	26%	35%	37%
Weighted base	(27)	(173)	(76)

28

had not given any previous thought to claiming, did in fact, make a claim (table 3.6).

Table 3.6 Claim action after follow up interview by extent of action taken previously

Claiming action after follow up	Extent of claim action described at follow up interview		
	Taken action	Thought about	No thought or action
	%	%	%
Claimed benefit after follow up interview	25	13	10
Still non-claimant by end of the study (or not known)	75	87	90
Total %	100	100	100
Base: All non-claimants at follow up (weighted)	24	58	101

PART II

A test of the Kerr threshold model

The threshold model

4.1 Introduction

One of the main aims of the study was to test the Kerr threshold model. This model attempts to define the decision processes involved in claiming and Kerr has argued that its advantage as a method lies in its predictive power. It predicts whether people will claim or not according to their responses to a set of predefined criteria. The prediction can then be checked against subsequent claiming behaviour. If the prediction is correct the reasons for not claiming posed by the model are validated.

The method was devised in response to a critique of previous studies which provided only post hoc rationalisations of non-claiming. Kerr argued that because the explanations could not be confirmed, by testing against behaviour, there was no verification that they were correct.

The threshold model was developed by Kerr in Glasgow and tested amongst one benefit group, eligible non-claimants of supplementary pensions. However, it has not been applied in a predictive sense to other benefit groups, as has been done in this study. This application raises two questions:

- can the model accurately predict claiming behaviour for other means tested benefits
- does it have equal application to all claim unit types

The remainder of this chapter will be devoted to considering these two questions. But first the method of application in this study is discussed.

4.2 The Kerr threshold model

The model consists of a series of steps, or decision thresholds, through which the prospective claimant must pass before finally arriving at the decision to apply for a benefit. It was developed using previous research findings in which general reasons for not claiming were translated into six conceptually distinct variables as outlined earlier (page 3). A second dimension in constructing the model was to consider the nature of linkages between the main variables. Previous research had shown that none of the individual variables alone explained claiming or non-claiming and that the variables appeared to be interrelated. The order of the thresholds was determined by logic, underpinned by psychological dissonance theory.[1] A diagramatic representation of the model is shown in figure 4.1. As will be seen, it is assumed that all the thresholds must be passed before a person will proceed to apply for a benefit.

---

(1) See Chapter 2 of Scott Kerr, *Making Ends Meet*, 1983.

Figure 4.1 Representation of the Kerr Threshold Model

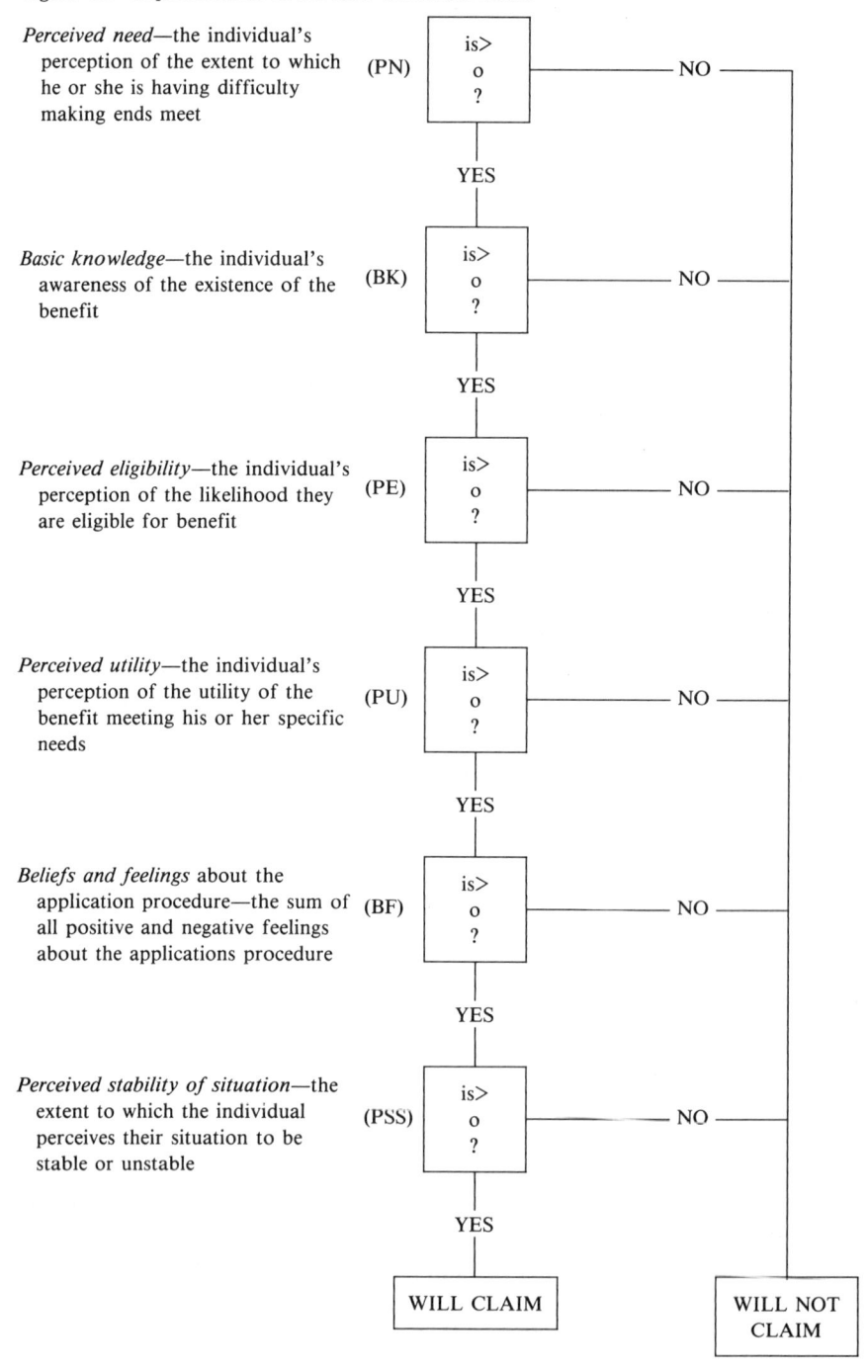

Perceived need—the individual's perception of the extent to which he or she is having difficulty making ends meet (PN) is>o? —— NO ——

YES

Basic knowledge—the individual's awareness of the existence of the benefit (BK) is>o? —— NO ——

YES

Perceived eligibility—the individual's perception of the likelihood they are eligible for benefit (PE) is>o? —— NO ——

YES

Perceived utility—the individual's perception of the utility of the benefit meeting his or her specific needs (PU) is>o? —— NO ——

YES

Beliefs and feelings about the application procedure—the sum of all positive and negative feelings about the applications procedure (BF) is>o? —— NO ——

YES

Perceived stability of situation—the extent to which the individual perceives their situation to be stable or unstable (PSS) is>o? —— NO ——

YES

| WILL CLAIM | WILL NOT CLAIM |

Method of applying the model

The method by which the model is applied is logically very simple. Each variable is represented by a question or series of questions. These involve two types of answer, either involving a scale or a simple positive or negative response. An example, as used by Kerr, is provided by the measure of perceived need. In this case, the respondent is shown a card on which a series of statements are shown. The respondents are asked to indicate which statements they think best apply to them:

ie: Which of the following statements applies to you:

No	1 Your income is lot more than your expenses
Perceived	2 Your income is a little more than your expenses
Need	3 Your income matches your expenses
Perceived	4 Your income is a little less than your expenses
Need	5 Your income is much less than your expenses

All those who responded with codes 1, 2 or 3 were taken to score negatively on perceived need; ie to have no perceived need, as shown in the diagram. Those who responded to codes 4 or 5 were taken to have a positive score.

The principle used in applying the model is that each threshold is tested sequentially. For example, those who score negatively on perceived need, that is do not perceive themselves to be in need, are predicted not to claim and taken out before the next threshold is applied. Those who perceive a need continue to the next threshold where the same procedure is applied. If the outcome on the second threshold is positive they continue to the next, and so on, until all the thresholds have been tested. If the score is positive on all the thresholds, the individual is predicted to claim. If, on the other hand, they score negatively on *any* threshold, they are predicted not to claim and hence drop out of the process.

Kerr measured only four of the thresholds in his study of supplementary pensioners. These were perceived need, (1st threshold) perceived utility (4th) beliefs and feelings (5th) and perceived stability of situation (6th). The other two, basic knowledge and perceived eligibility, were not measured because they were considered to be 'controlled' in the experimental sense. Kerr argued that, because respondents had received a letter informing them of their entitlement, basic knowledge and perceived eligibility were positive in all cases. The measures used by Kerr for the other four thresholds and the methods by which they were applied are detailed in 'Making Ends Meet', Kerr's report on his study.

4.3 The application of the model in the present study

The model used in the present study was, in principle, the same as Kerr's. There were, however, some modifications to the application of the model which concerned both the *number* of thresholds measured and the *form of measurement* used. These modifications were introduced, partly because of differences between the designs of the two studies but also because it was felt that refinements to the measures could be made.

The number of thresholds measured

In the present study, all six thresholds were measured. It was not assumed that either basic knowledge or perceived eligibility existed, unless there was some affirmation to this effect. There were two reasons why this was felt necessary, both of which related to the design of the study. First, not all of the main sample remembered receiving the letter which informed them of their possible eligibility. Whether this was because it did not arrive, or because it had been forgotten or simply dismissed on arrival, cannot be checked. Either way, knowledge and perceived eligibility were uncertain. Second, the supplementary sample were not sent a letter at the end of the Hackney Benefit Study (see chapter 2) so that there was no question that either prior knowledge or perceived eligibility could be assumed. Indeed as we see later, there were a small number of people who said they had never heard of the benefit for which they were thought to be entitled and rather more who did not perceive themselves as eligible.

The measurement of the thresholds

A brief description of the way the individual thresholds were measured is given below. It is important to note that none of them were measured in exactly the same form as in the Kerr study although the underlying principles were identical. In all cases it was felt that changes could be made which would help to refine the individual measures.

Perceived need was derived from two items concerning perceptions of the extent to which the person's income met their expenses. Perceived need was said to exist if the following conditions were met.

> PN: Income was less than expenses
>
> or
>
> Income just matched expenses but there was some achnowledged difficulty in managing.

Basic knowledge was confirmed if the person said they knew the name of the benefit concerned.

> BK: Had heard of the benefit for which a claim was being discussed.

Perceived eligibility was measured differently for the two sample groups because of their different treatment in the study design.

The measure used was defined as follows:

> PE: (Main Sample): Remembered receiving letter or made positive statement about eligibility.
>
> PE: (Supplementary Sample): Made positive statement about eligibility or no negative statement about eligibility.

Two points should be made about this measure, both of which are said with hindsight. First, we believe it was ill advised not to include a systematic measure of perceived eligibility on the questionnaire. The absence of this left us dependent on spontaneous comments about the person's perception from which comprehensive judgements cannot be made (ie no assumptions can be made when comments are simply absent). The second, and related point, is that it was inappropriate to treat the two samples differently on this particular measure. We return to both these points in the next section, but the inadequacies of this measure should be noted here.

Perceived utility

The measure of perceived utility was derived from two questions concerning the amount of money people thought they would get if they claimed; and the minimum amount they thought worth claiming. If the first amount was larger than the second, they were assumed to perceive some utility.

> PU: Amount of benefit likely to receive was greater than minimum amount worth claiming.

Beliefs and feelings

As in the Kerr study, a battery of questions was asked about 'beliefs and feelings' about the claim process. These differed slightly for the three benefits (because of differences in the claim procedures) but covered broadly the same issues. On all such items, respondents were asked if they had a strong feeling about a particular aspect of the procedure and if so, to explain what their feelings were. The response was rated on a seven point scale ranging from +3 through 0 to −3.

The measure of 'beliefs and feelings' was derived from a subset of the full battery of questions. The sum of the scores on these items was used to provide the measure of beliefs and feelings about the claim process.

> BF: Positive or neutral beliefs and feelings about claim process (ie summed score of 0, +1, +2 or +3)

Perceived stability of situation

This measure was derived from a question about anticipated changes in financial circumstances and from spontaneous commentary about any circumstantial change. Perceived stability was said to exist if the following conditions were met.

> PSS: Does not expect financial circumstances to improve
> or
> no spontaneous mention of any major change in circumstances

The test sample

The model was applied only to people who were still *non-claimants* at the time of follow-up interview (ie in the summer of 1984). It was not possible to include the 65 people who had made a claim between the main Hackney study and this time since their perceptions or feelings might very well have changed *because of* the claim itself (ie perceived eligibility, beliefs and feelings about the claim process). We should note however that by removing this tier of claimants, we were dealing with those who were perhaps more resistant to claim, certainly amongst the larger main sample (ie they had not claimed despite having had a full interview in the main study and a letter).

4.4 Testing the model: the results

Predicted claimants and non-claimants

As previously discussed, the model was tested among 119[1] non-claimants who had not claimed the benefit for which they were eligible by the time of the follow-up interview. Of these, 20 (17%) were predicted to claim and 99 (83%) were predicted as non-claimants. The proportions predicted to claim were very similar for the two samples and among the three benefit groups (table 4.1).

Table 4.1 Predictions from Kerr model by sample type and benefit group

		Predicted Claimant	Predicted Non-claimant	Total %	*Base:* All Non-claimants at follow-up interview (unweighted)
Main sample	%	16	84	100	85
Supplementary sample	%	18	82	100	34
Main benefit					
HB	%	17	83	100	65
SB	%	16	84	100	49
FIS	No	(1)	(4)	—	5
Total	%	17	83		119

In terms of individual thresholds, the largest proportion of non-claiming was attributed to the first threshold—namely a lack of perceived need (figure 4.2). Altogether, 46% of those tested were predicted not to claim because they scored negatively on this measure. A further small proportion (3%) were predicted not to claim because they apparently did not know of the benefits existence, while 11% had negative views about their own eligibility.

Of the 40% who reached the fourth threshold, 5% did not think the benefit they would get was of sufficient value to make it worth claiming and thus failed on 'perceived utility'. At threshold five, 'beliefs and feelings', a sizeable drop out ocurred (15%) because of negative views or feelings about the claiming procedure. This left only one fifth of the sample to arrive at threshold six at which a further small proportion (3%) were predicted not to claim. The remaining 17%, having passed through all six thresholds, were predicted to claim.

The proportions passing each threshold are of course dependent on the order in which the thresholds occur. If for example, beliefs and feelings had appeared at an earlier stage of the model, it may well have been that the proportions predicted not to claim because of negative attitudes towards the claim procedure would have been higher. It is therefore important not to put too much weight on the numbers dropping out at each stage, since the predictive power of the model lies in the final outcome. However since the order was the same for all individuals tested, it is possible to consider whether

---

(1) Unweighted figures have been used in all significance tests of the model.

Figure 4.2 The threshold model: predictions and outcome at individual thresholds

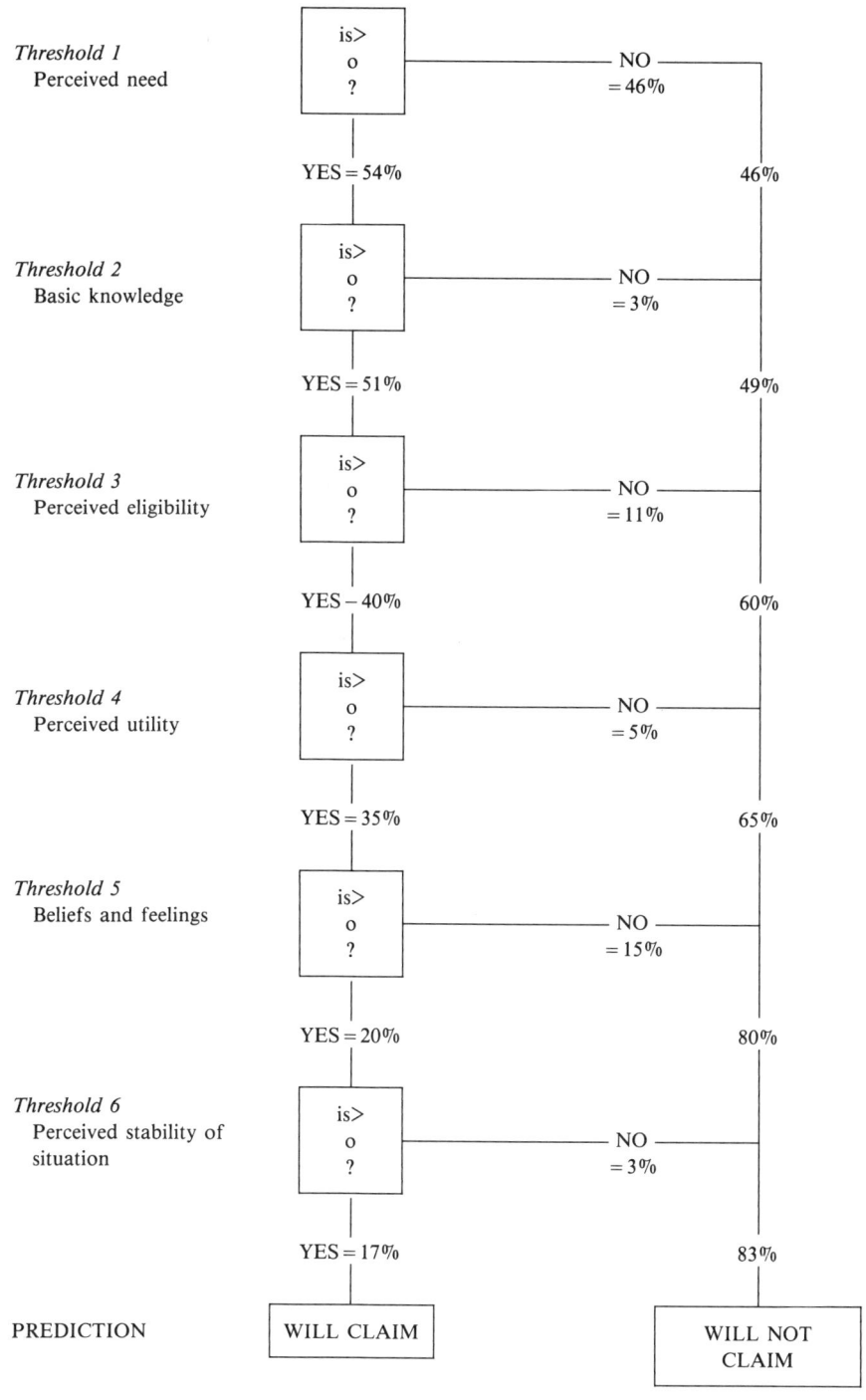

```
                         ┌──────┐
Threshold 1              │ is>  │
Perceived need           │  o   │──────── NO ─────────┐
                         │  ?   │        = 46%        │
                         └──────┘                     │
                            │                         │
                       YES = 54%                     46%

                         ┌──────┐
Threshold 2              │ is>  │
Basic knowledge          │  o   │──────── NO ─────────┤
                         │  ?   │        = 3%         │
                         └──────┘                     │
                            │                         │
                       YES = 51%                     49%

                         ┌──────┐
Threshold 3              │ is>  │
Perceived eligibility    │  o   │──────── NO ─────────┤
                         │  ?   │        = 11%        │
                         └──────┘                     │
                            │                         │
                       YES – 40%                     60%

                         ┌──────┐
Threshold 4              │ is>  │
Perceived utility        │  o   │──────── NO ─────────┤
                         │  ?   │        = 5%         │
                         └──────┘                     │
                            │                         │
                       YES = 35%                     65%

                         ┌──────┐
Threshold 5              │ is>  │
Beliefs and feelings     │  o   │──────── NO ─────────┤
                         │  ?   │        = 15%        │
                         └──────┘                     │
                            │                         │
                       YES = 20%                     80%

                         ┌──────┐
Threshold 6              │ is>  │
Perceived stability of   │  o   │──────── NO ─────────┤
situation                │  ?   │        = 3%         │
                         └──────┘                     │
                            │                         │
                       YES = 17%                     83%

                      ┌───────────┐              ┌───────────┐
PREDICTION            │WILL CLAIM │              │ WILL NOT  │
                      └───────────┘              │   CLAIM   │
                                                 └───────────┘
```

BASE: All non-claimants at time of follow-up interview (119 unweighted)

the pattern of progress through the model varies for the different sample and benefit groups (table 4.2).

Table 4.2 Proportions predicted to claim at each threshold, by benefit group

Proportions passing thresholds concerning	Benefit group		
	HB	SB	FIS
	%	%	No.
Perceived need	46	65	(2)
Basic knowledge	45	61	(2)
Perceived eligibility	43	39	(1)
Perceived utility	35	37	(1)
Beliefs and feelings	20	20	(1)
Perceived stability	17	16	(1)
Base: Non-claimants at time of follow-up (unweighted)	65	49	5

The comparison between benefit groups and sample types does show differences in the internal working of the model, although not, in the overall proportions predicted to claim. Those eligible for supplementary benefit were less likely than HB (or FIS) non-claimants to fall at the first threshold because of a lack of perceived need. The pattern however became very similar to HB again after the perceived eligibility threshold, which over one fifth of the SB non-claimants failed to pass.

Comparison of predictions with claiming behaviour

In order to check the correctness of the predictions, the output from the model was compared with information from the record check. It will be remembered that, one year after the follow-up interview, benefit records were checked to see if a claim had been made. The results of this comparison are as shown in table 4.3.

Table 4.3 Predictions from Kerr model by claiming behaviour
(as shown in record check)

	Claimed benefit	Did not claim benefit	Record check not possible	Total
	No.	No.	No.	No.
Predicted to claim	8	10	2	20
Predicted not to claim	7	75	17	99
Base: Non-claimants at time of follow up interview	15	85	19	119

40

If we consider the 104[1] cases for which the record check could be made, we find that the association between predicted claiming behaviour and actual behaviour is highly significant (see table 4.4). This suggests that the model does have some ability to predict whether or not a claim for benefit will be made. The model's ability to predict a correct outcome is slightly better for the main sample ($p<.02$) than for the supplementary sample ($p<.10$) and much better for SB ($p<.02$) than for HB ($p<.20$). Indeed for HB, there is only slight evidence of any association between prediction and outcome.

Overall 83% of cases were correctly predicted by the model. However this percentage was very different for those predicted to claim (44% correct pre-

Table 4.4 Predictions from Kerr model by claiming behaviour

All non-claimants (for whom record check could be made)

Predictions from model	Claimed benefit	Did not claim benefit	Total
Predicted to claim	8	10	18
Predicted not to claim	7	75	82

Total
$\chi^2 = 12.243$ (significance = $p<.001$)

Sample types

Main sample

	Claimed Benefit	Did not claim	Total
Predicted to claim	5	7	12
Predicted not to claim	5	54	59
Total	10	61	71

$\chi^2 = 6.54$ (significance = $p<.02$)

Supplementary Sample

	Claimed Benefit	Did not claim	Total
Predicted to claim	3	3	6
Predicted not to claim	2	21	23
Total	5	24	29

$\chi^2 = 3.163$ (significance = $p<.10$)

Benefit groups

HB non claimants

	Claimed Benefit	Did not claim	Total
Predicted to claim	3	7	10
Predicted not to claim	4	41	45
Total	7	48	55

$\chi^2 = 1.657$ (significance = $p<.20$)

SB non claimants

	Claimed Benefit	Did not claim	Total
Predicted to claim	4	3	7
Predicted not to claim	3	31	34
Total	7	34	41

$\chi^2 = 6.464$ (significance = $p<.02$)

Note: The above figures include cases where eligibility at the time of the follow-up interview was either uncertain or had changed. An analysis identical to the above was undertaken on certainly eligible cases (ie excluding any non-eligible or uncertain). The results are compatible with the above analysis.

(1) There were 19 cases where a record check was not possible (ie permission was not given, signed form was missing etc.) These have not been included in the test of the Kerr model. We should note however that other evidence collected in the questionnaire would suggest that the great majority of these claim units would not have claimed, as the model predicts.

dictions) and those predicted not to claim (91% correct). Although the proportion of correct predictions *not* to claim is identical for both HB and SB (ie 91%), the model appears to be less good at successful predicting HB claimants (30% correct) than SB claimants (57%) (table 4.4).

It is also important to note that the model appears to work better for certain subgroups than others (table 4.5). For example the proportion of correct predictions was best for those aged between 50 and pensionable age, a group we previously identified as claim resistant. There was also a notable difference between claim units with dependent children (65%) and those without (96%) in the extent to which the model correctly predicted behaviour. Although most of the differences shown would not be statistically significant (because of the small sample sizes) this does not mean they have to be ignored. Indeed, these differences suggest that the predictive power of the model does not operate uniformly among all groups.

Although there are differences in the predictive power of the model, we can conclude that it has identified key elements in the decision process surrounding benefit claims. Indeed, as far as decisions *not* to claim either SB or HB are concerned, the model is correct nine times out of ten. This would suggest that the variables contained within the model, when negatively aspected, include most of the major inhibitors to a claim.

These findings are important in four respects. First, they confirm that non-take up is the result of a number of different factors. There is no one single cause which can explain claiming or non-claiming behaviour. Second, the various factors that are included are in part to do with the benefit system,

Table 4.5 Outcome of predictions from Kerr model by characteristics of claim units

Characteristics of Claim units		Prediction Correct	Prediction Incorrect	Total %	Base: Non-claimants at follow-up interview(1)
Age of head of claim unit					
Under 50	%	72	28	100	46
50 to pensionable age	%	90	11	100	46
Pensionable age or over	%	78	22	100	59
Non pensioners					
With dependent children	%	65	35	100	40
No dependent children	%	96	4	100	48
Activity status					
Full time employment	%	77	13	100	70
Part time employment	No.	(6)	(2)	100	8
Unemployed	No.	(5)	—	100	5
Retired	%	81	19	100	57
Other	No	(10)	(2)	100	12
Tenure					
Owner occupier	No	(15)	—	—	15
Council tenant	%	82	18	100	101
Other tenant	%	65	35	100	34

(1) Only those cases where the prediction could be checked have been included in this table.

and the way it is administered; and, in part, to do with the individual and his or her beliefs, feelings or circumstances. Third, the nature of the constructs within the model suggest that complex processes are at work. Why, for example, do such high proportions of non-claimants lack a perception of 'need' when by statutory definition their 'needs' outweigh, their resources'. Finally, and perhaps most important, it would seem that the processses at work are not benefit specific and have more general application to those which contain a means tested component.

In the next section of the report we will consider the nature of the processes contained within the threshold model and how these negative influences might be overcome. Before doing so, however, it is useful to examine further the cases which were incorrectly predicted by the Kerr model. In particular, it is important to try to clarify why the model is better at predicting non-claimants than claimants and why it does not have equally good results for all types of claimant groups.

5 Failed cases

We have already shown that the claiming behaviour of 17 people was incorrectly predicted by the model. Of these 10 were non-claimants (predicted to claim) and 7 were claimants (predicted not to claim). Subsequent analysis of these groups, including an inspection of the questionnaires, suggests three reasons why incorrect predictions may have occurred. These are:

- the measurement of individual thresholds
- the relative strength of factors operating within the model
- the importance of factors not covered by the model.

The measurement of individual thresholds

The evidence suggests that the methods by which two of the threshold constructs were measured may account for a proportion of the failed cases. The thresholds concerned are 'perceived eligibility' and 'beliefs and feelings' about the claiming procedure.

Perceived eligibility For those claimants who had received a letter about their possible entitlement, it was assumed that a 'perception' of eligibility existed.[1] It was evident, however, that some of the claim units wrongly predicted *to claim* expressed real uncertainty about the likelihood of a successful outcome even in cases where a letter had been received. In other words the advice they had received about possible eligibility had been overridden by other doubts, feelings or misconceptions. For example:

> 'I don't think we are due for it as we are working...My husband says in no way are we due for it'
>
> (HB non-claimant)

> 'I don't think I'd get it because I'm working part time'
>
> (SB non-claimant)

---

(1) This procedure was similar to that used by Kerr in the original developmental study.

In all cases these feelings of uncertainty were held by people in full or part time employment, all but one of whom were also families with dependent children.

Although it is possible that a letter from a non-official agency did not provide sufficient confirmation to overcome such misgivings, it seems likely that the process is more generalisable. That is, certain beliefs or feelings will always prevail over information people are given about their eligibility, unless of course it is part of the claim process itself. We would also suggest that while there will be some people who hold genuine misconceptions, there will be others for whom underlying attitudes have affected their willingness to perceive themselves as eligible. This is a point we shall return to in the next chapter.

It will be remembered that the measurement of this threshold was different for the main and the supplementary sample (see page 25). The failed cases in the main sample show that had we taken account of negative views about elibigility (as was done for the supplementary sample), then three more cases would have been correctly predicted as 'non-claimants' by the threshold model. However, the use of spontaneous comments is not the ideal solution. If a question about perceived eligibility (and the certainty with which it was felt) had been systematically asked of all respondents, we believe the measurement of this threshold would have been improved.

Beliefs and feelings The other measure about which we have some doubts, although they are less serious, concerns beliefs and feelings about the claiming procedure. Our main reservation is that the summation of scores across a number of items may have a flattening effect on any strongly negative or positive views (eg two very negative scores and eight mildly positive, would end up as an overall positive score). It may be however that the aspect about which negative views are held is crucially important. There was certainly one failed case (predicted to claim) where the average beliefs and feelings score was around zero, but one aspect (providing information about income) was very negatively valued.[1] Indeed the respondent concerned was explicit about the fact that this was the deterrent to claiming. It may be, therefore, that extremely negative views on any aspect need to be taken into account as well as the average score.

Relative strength of factors within the model

There is some evidence to suggest that if the score on certain threshold constructs is particularly high, then the other thresholds may be immaterial in predicting a claim. Of particular relevance in this context is 'perceived need'. Among the cases wrongly predicted as non-claimants, there were five cases where perceived need was very high. In each case, however, they failed on other thresholds, most commonly 'beliefs and feelings'. These non-claimants had made a claim because of the difficulties they were having in managing, despite holding quite negative views about the claim procedure they would have to go through. Similarly, there was one case where serious doubts about eligibility were expressed but the level of perceived need led them to make

---

(1) We should note that the same pattern of responses was not found among a sample of *correctly* predicted non-claimants, where there tended to be negative scores on several items.

enquiries and hence to make a claim. This overriding force of 'perceived need' appeared in all types of claim units.

Although this problem could possibly be overcome technically (ie by taking some account of the level of need expressed in the measurement of the threshold) we suspect that the process is more complex. We believe it is more likely that in some cases the level of need will overcome inhibiting factors and in other cases it will not. Indeed, this is to some extent confirmed by cases *correctly* predicted as non-claimants where high levels of need, equivalent to those described, were overwhelmed by very negative feelings about the claim process.

The importance of other factors

There were five failed cases for which the reason for failure was difficult to find. All of them were non-claimants who had been predicted to claim and had not done so. In each case, however, they had passed all the thresholds and all but one or two appeared to be on the brink of claiming (ie they said that they thought they definitely would or very probably would claim). Why, then, had they not done so?

Although we cannot be certain about the answer to this, we believe the roots lie in generally unfavourable attitudes towards the idea of benefit support. In other words, there is an underlying feeling about being on a 'means tested' benefit that has eventually inhibited the claim. Such attitudes are not necessarily reflected in the model constructs nor indeed captured by questions asked in other parts of the questionnaire (ie questions on benefits being a 'right or a charity').

Our evidence for believing these underlying attitudes may have effected the eventual decision to claim is two-fold: First, other research, particularly that which has used exploratory rather than structured forms of questioning, has shown that in some cases such attitudes can be all pervasive (see, for example, Ritchie and Matthews, 1983). Secondly, these 'unexplained' cases are confined to two types of claim units—pensioners and two parent families. In both cases, there is other documented evidence which suggest that these groups may view the receipt of state benefits negatively (ie because of the loss of independence or 'pride' for pensioners, because of a threat to the 'breadwinner' status for two parent families).

We cannot, of course, be certain about any of these reasons for failure. They are simply our judgements based on reviewing the questionnaire information of the cases involved. However, it is worth recording a summary of the incidence of the judged reasons for failure in relation to the prediction that was made. It was as follows:

Judged cause of 'failure'	Wrongly predicted to claim	Wrongly predicted as non-claimant
Measurement of individual thresholds	oooo	
Relative force of factor		ooooo
Missing factor(s)	oooooo	
Uncertain cases		oo
Total	10	7

It would be rare for any behavioural model to accurately predict all outcomes and the failure of these cases must be seen in this light. It is also the case that some of the suggested causes of failure are based on judgements which cannot be proven from the questionnaire data. Nevertheless the failed cases have gone some way to explaining why the model may be less good at predicting claimants than non-claimants and is not uniformly successful amongst all claim unit types. First, the summary above shows that there are two possible reasons why an incorrect prediction to claim might be made. In other words, two of the possible weaknesses might operate when a prediction to claim is being made, as opposed to only one for the prediction not to claim. We believe, however, that both of these might be solved by refinements or additions to the model. Secondly, it is evident that certain groups, such as two parent families, may be prone to all three causes of failure. This in turn might explain some of the lower success rates detailed in table 4.5.

4.6 Summary

This chapter has shown that the Kerr threshold model has a high success rate in predicting non-claimants. Although it appears to be less good at predicting claimants and does not work uniformly well for all benefits and claim unit types, we believe that some of the reasons for this have been illuminated by the failed cases. In our view the model has not only proved itself as a strong predictor, it has provided invaluable insight into many of the key elements which negatively influence the decision to claim.

PART III

Crossing the threshold towards a claim

The balance of forces

Introduction

The previous chapter has shown that the Kerr decision model has a strong predictive power in explaining claiming behaviour. Although we would suggest certain refinements to the model we believe that the premises on which it is built are correct. That is, there are a number of factors operating in the decision making process and certain key thresholds need to be crossed before a decision to claim will be made. These we believe are crucial elements in understanding the claim, or non-claiming, process.

To extend our understanding of how the model works we need to explore the influential factors that surround it. Some of these are embedded within the model itself (eg perceived need), others are external forces which might inhibit or encourage movement across thresholds (eg desirability of 'independence' or 'managing'). Only by understanding the factors which stop people crossing thresholds, or more importantly, move people across them, can we begin to understand what can be done to improve take up levels.

When considering the nature of the influences surrounding claim decisions, it is important to bear in mind that a process of 'trade off' may be at work. This representation, which was described in the review of previous research, suggests that when people are making a decision about a claim they will weigh up, consciously or unconsciously, the advantages against the disadvantages. It is our view that this mechanism of 'trade off' can occur not only in relation to the decision process as a whole, but also at individual thresholds. In other words, whether or not a person passes across a particular threshold will in itself be a result of the balance of forces that surround it.

Our purpose in introducing the notion of a trade off between opposing forces is three fold. First, from a purely pragmatic point of view, it helps to clarify where action is needed. If take up is to be increased then the positive forces need to be increased or reinforced and the negative forces decreased or removed. Second, it enables the whole range of influences to be considered, and not just those embedded within the decision process itself. For example, social approval may not be a necessary requisite for a person to decide to claim. It may however be highly influential in counteracting any negative feelings about being in receipt of benefits. In other words, it may be the necessary force that moves a person across one or more of the thresholds. The third reason relates to a reservation about the threshold model noted earlier. It was suggested in the previous chapter that there could be circumstances where the relative weight of one factor is so strong that all others become irrelevant. In such cases, it is the balance of forces, rather than the passing of thresholds, which will produce the decision to claim.

In the next two chapters we shall consider the negative and positive forces at work, with the aim of increasing understanding of their nature and influence. In doing this, we are faced with certain presentational problems since the various factors involved can have either a positive or negative influence (ie perceived need encourages a claim, lack of perceived need inhibits a claim). In order to avoid repetition we have chosen to look first at the nature of the negative elements and then at the factors which can help to overcome them.

The negative forces: factors which discourage take-up

In this chapter we shall consider the negative forces which inhibit movement across thresholds and thus prevent claims occurring. The factors we shall be discussing are not new to take up research. Indeed, most of them were referred to in the first chapter. Our purpose in discussing them again here is two fold. First, there is an important link to be drawn between the evidence provided by the Kerr model and the influences that surround it. We have seen that the Kerr model has a high success rate in predicting non-claimants. We now need to unlock the components of the model to examine the nature of the factors that work within it. Second, the present study provided the rare opportunity to examine the import of the various influences on claiming across more than one benefit and for different types of claim unit. This latter feature also provides an important focus for the discussion which follows.

In the main, the analysis presented in this chapter is confined to people who were still non-claimants at the time of the follow up interview. This is the same group to which the test of the Kerr model was applied. Occasionally, however, it is useful to compare the views of this group with those who had became claimants by the time they were interviewed for this study. We shall refer to the two groups as 'non-claimants' and 'claimants' although it has to be remembered that they were all non-claimants when the Hackney Benefit Study was undertaken.

5.1 Lack of perceived need

It has been shown that some acknowledgement of being in 'need' is crucial to the decision to claim a benefit. Yet there are many eligible non-claimants who do not see themselves as being in need and thus do not make a claim. This is puzzling since they are officially defined as being in 'need' of additional income. By objective criteria, their income does not meet their expenses, sometimes by quite a wide margin, and yet they do not perceive it this way. We found for example that *half* of those who were assessed as being eligible for £5.00 or more of unclaimed benefit, said their income met their expenses, or, even, was greater. It is important to understand why.

The desire to manage

For many people, the lack of a perceived need is related to a desire to manage. What managing means varies for different people but almost universally involves cutting out some items of expenditure (eg holidays, entertainment, presents, clothes, home improvements etc) and cutting down on others (eg food, heating, hot water, transport fares etc). In essence, therefore, managing is being able to pay essential bills (eg rent, fuel etc) and then adapting remaining expenditure to the required level.[1]

To an extent, all households have to 'manage' their expenditure so that it does not exceed their income. Where these eligible non-claimants differ, however, is in the level of curtailment, and even deprivation, that it requires. Indeed over a third of the non-claimants admitted to having considerable difficulties in managing and rather more were cutting back on food and heating as well as many less essential items. This picture was much the same for both HB and SB non-claimants (table 5.1).

NON-CLAIMANTS AT FOLLOW UP

Table 5.1 Level of managing; items of expenditure which have been cut back by benefit group

Managing level	HB	SB	FIS	TOTAL
			No.	
Finds managing on present income				
—a great struggle	10%	13%	(3)	13%
—pretty hard	24%	19%	—	22%
—a little difficult	46%	44%	(2)	45%
Has no trouble managing	19%	25%	—	20%
Items on which cut back in last few months				
Electricity	50%	62%	(3)	54%
Heating	37%	43%	(2)	39%
Meat	48%	47%	(3)	48%
Other food	38%	31%	(1)	35%
Clothes or shoes	60%	53%	(5)	59%
Visits to relatives	24%	24%	—	24%
Entertainment	28%	35%	(3)	31%
Not cut down on anything	14%	11%	—	13%
Base: Non claimants				
weighted	124	54	—	183
unweighted	65	49	5	119

Although the desire to manage often appears to be rooted in the wish to avoid dependence, it can manifest itself in different ways. These are illustrated below:

Pride in 'managing'

It is clear that some people positively enjoy, and take a pride in, managing on the income they have. An example, drawn from some in-depth interviews,[2] illustrates this circumstance well. The respondent was a retired

---

(1) For a more detailed discussion of the nature of 'managing', see Ritchie and Matthews, 1983.
(2) Some in-depth interviews with eligible non-claimants were carried out on the main Hackney study and have been used to provide more detailed illustrative evidence.

woman, living with a single son. She described proudly how she obtained her clothes from jumble sales and rejoiced happily in the nick name 'second hand Rose'. She explained that her needs were simple:

> 'I've got enough. I've got very simple tastes. I don't smoke or drink or go to the cinema. My daughter does my hair so that doesn't cost me anything. I often go to jumble sales. I prefer shopping at jumble sales than to shop.'

However, as will be constantly stressed throughout this section, the lack of perceived need was conditioned by other factors. It was associated with a strongly held value placed on independence and some very negative feelings about the claim process. So strong was the importance of independence in the case of the non-claimant above that she said she would prefer to go without eating than borrow money.

> 'I've always cut my coat according to the cloth. I mean if I had to go without, if I had to without a meal or something I would. I would never—how can I explain it—I would never be in debt or borrow money.'

When asked if she would ever consider claiming supplementary benefit, she answered as follows:

> 'Well I'd have to be in a very great need. If I've got to go somewhere and fill in my life story, perhaps waiting in a queue with other unfortunate people who are applying for the same thing. I would have to be in a very great need before I would. I would use my savings first. I've heard of people asking for help and being refused and it always put me off. I would hate myself really. I'd rather do anything or mostly anything than go to one of those officials and ask for help.'

It is clear that in the face of such strong feelings it would be difficult and possibly undesirable to try and influence a change, even if that were possible.

Getting by

In some cases, the desire to manage was not accompanied by such a strong sense of well being financially. It is more a case of doing without to get by rather than a positive pride in managing. It is in these cases that other forces may have an influence to prompt a claim. An example is provided by a young single parent of 21 years. Her partner (the child's father) had left the year previously, leaving her with considerable rent arrears. She also had to pick up bills for gas and electricity which he had previously paid out of his income. She was in full time work and entitled to housing benefit. She had a poor understanding of the benefit system, but rather than investigate it further she managed by cutting back. For example, she had reduced her use of electricity:

> 'Before we used the electricity but now we are always using gas because it is more economical. It's only when we go to bed that we put on the electricity because it's more economical.'

She had £600 in rent arrears and this presented her with some anxiety, as well as an appreciation that she had difficulty in managing. However, she was still reluctant to make a claim, and so long as she felt could keep her head just above water, did not seem likely to go forward.

> 'Well that's me you see... There are lots of things I don't get. Once I can get something to keep me going I just get by you see.'

Alternatives to benefits

Another way of managing to avoid a claim for benefits is to find some alternative means of increasing income. For most people this is not easy but for those in employment, working overtime or increasing the number of part time hours is a possible option. This was the preferred choice made by a single parent with an 11 year old son even though the pay was low and the hours difficult. In this case the desire to manage was prompted by a strong feeling against claiming supplementary benefit, which stemmed from an earlier experience of the benefit system. She had been on supplementary benefit when her son was first born, and had disliked the experience:

> 'They came and asked me so many questions, they told me several people come to me, "You're jumping in and out of bed" They said some terrible things to me. I'm not exaggerating. I felt as though I was begging.'

More recently she had received help from her mother who had died the year earlier. Now her son was at secondary school she might be able to work longer hours.

> 'Well I'd like to work longer hours now as a matter of fact I've asked because Michael now goes to secondary school. It's not easy though because they are cutting back. My hours have been cut rather than added to...'

But for her the decision to claim was in balance. She was weighing up the merits of a claim against alternative sources of income. With the right encouragement she might be moved towards claiming because this was legitimised by, and certainly more compatible with, her son's needs. When told she would almost certainly be eligible for FIS, she said she would claim it 'if I was sure I was eligible.' But she would not claim supplementary benefit because of her earlier experience.

These examples illustrate that a desire to 'manage' can result from a variety of factors, some of which are connected with the benefit system itself and some with much more deep rooted values. In many cases, managing means managing without the help of state support, whatever difficulties that may bring.

In this context, it is of interest to note some variance between groups in their attitudes towards 'managing' and 'need'. Table 5.2 shows how different types of claim units responded to questions about 'perceived need' (as defined in the threshold model) and to a question on how difficult they found it to manage. Although the levels of perceived need remain at a consistent level, there do appear to be some differences in the extent to which the claim units felt they were managing. Two points are worthy of note. First, it seems that families with dependent children are having the most difficulty in making ends meet, with 50% saying managing was hard or a great struggle and only 5% saying they had no difficulties at all. This is also reflected in the cut backs in expenditure they have had to make.

Second, it seems that pensioners are a little less likely than the non-pensioner groups to find managing hard or a great struggle. Although this could be simply reflecting a semantic difference, it is more likely to reflect differences in the demands on, or expectations of, their expenditure. It could also be the case, of course, that they are more reluctant to admit to serious

Table 5.2 Perceptions of need and levels of managing by composition of claim unit

Perceived need and levels of managing	Non-Pensioners		Pensioners	
	Without dep. child	With dep. child	Single	Married
Perceived need (as defined in threshold model)[1]	53%	57%	52%	55%
Finds managing				
—a little difficult	42%	45%	52%	44%
—hard or a great struggle	37%	50%	25%	23%
—has no difficulties managing	21%	5%	23%	23%
Items cut back in last few months				
—Electricity	55%	57%	50%	56%
—Heating	32%	52%	49%	33%
—Meat	48%	50%	52%	38%
—Other food	25%	41%	37%	44%
—Clothes or shoes	65%	66%	51%	59%
—Visits to relatives	25%	34%	18%	13%
—Entertainment	42%	32%	18%	28%
Not cut down on anything	10%	5%	25%	13%
Base: Non-claimants				
weighted	60	44	46	33
unweighted	36	27	31	25

(1) For definition, see page 34

Table 5.3 Perceptions of need and levels of managing among claimants and non-claimants, by benefit group

Perceptions of need and levels of managing	HB	SB	FIS	TOTAL
Proportions with *perceived need*				
—claimants	68%	93%	(4)	75%
—non-claimants	49%	65%	(2)	54%
Proportions who *find managing hard or a great struggle*				
—claimants	53%	70%	(3)	59%
—non-claimants	34%	32%	(3)	34%
Base: (Weighted)				
claimants	68	27	4	99
non-claimants	124	54	5	183

difficulties in managing since this would bring them closer to the threshold of being in 'need'.

A final point that should be noted here is that the people who had already claimed benefit, by the time of the follow-up study, were more likely to perceive themselves as in need and to feel they had quite serious difficulties in managing when they were interviewed than those who were still non claimants (see table 5.3). In theory, this is the reverse of what might be expected. It might be supposed that people who have made the claim, and thus brought themselves above the official level of 'need' should be showing lower, rather than higher, proportions of perceived need than non-claimants. They should also, in theory, be finding it easier to manage than the non-claimants. The fact that the findings are quite the opposite lends support to the view that perceptions of need are highly subjective and greatly affected by other attitudes, particularly those concerning the idea of income support. In other words if people do not want to claim benefits they will be reluctant to admit they have any difficulties in managing so that they would avoid feeling in 'need'. We shall return to this point in the next chapter when we consider the forces which appear to have a positive influence of claiming.

5.2 Uncertainty about entitlement

Basic knowledge

Five percent[1] of the non-claimants had not heard of the benefit for which they were eligible. Although this is a small percentage, the people concerned tend to be clustered, mainly amongst pensioners and among single non-pensioner households. However, the great majority of the non-claimants knew of the benefit, at least by name, but their grasp of the conditions for eligibility, or what was involved in getting it, was often much more hazy. The case of one 73 year old widower is illustrative:

> Mr James was a home owner, unable to read and write. He is currently receiving the state retirement pension but also eligible for SB. He had recently suffered a heart attack and was on tablets that made him dizzy and gave him difficulty walking.
>
> He had never claimed before and never been to a social security office although he had heard of benefits on the TV and radio. He had no knowledge of the benefit procedure or of his own entitlement. He had no idea of what he might be eligible for. He thought he would be ineligible for housing benefit (to which he was also entitled) because he owned his own home.
>
> Although he felt he 'should be entitled to something', he was not certain, and this was an obstacle to claiming. Despite suggesting he would be 'very likely to claim in the near future', he said if he was turned down he would never call again.
>
> Mr James had not claimed at the end of the study.

It is in cases like this, and many others encountered, that a lack of knowledge and uncertainty about entitlement shade together to produce doubts about eligibility. A lack of perceived eligibility therefore becomes an important inhibitor to a claim.

Lack of perceived eligibility

Almost half of the non-claimants expressed some doubts about their eligibility during the course of the interview. This is a much higher figure than

---

(1) This percentage is slightly higher than the one shown in the Kerr model (3%). This is because the additional 2% had already failed to pass the first threshold of perceived need.

was indicated by the Kerr model where only 11% were predicted not to claim because of a lack of perceived eligibility. There are two reasons for this apparent inconsistency, both of which contain important findings in themselves. The first concerns the structural order of the Kerr model. Many of the people who had doubts about eligibility had already dropped out of the model (predicted as non-claimants) because of a lack of perceived need. This suggests there is some relationship between a lack of perceived need and uncertainty about entitlement, as indeed is the case. Over half (55%) of the people who had a lack of perceived eligibility (as defined in the Kerr model) did not perceive themselves in need and had therefore been predicted not to claim at the first threshold.

The second reason concerns problems with the measurement of perceived eligibility in the threshold model which have already been discussed (see page 42). As was noted before, it was assumed that people who had received the letter, telling them of their entitlement, could be assumed to perceive themselves as eligible. This is not at all the case. Indeed, almost half of those who received the letter expressed some doubts during the course of the interview. For the purpose of the discussion which follows we shall look at this wider group of people who hold some uncertainties about their eligibility. As we noted previously, this uncertainty was picked up through spontaneous comments made during the interview and not in response to a structured question.

It is important to look first at whether there are particular groups of non-claimants who display more uncertainty about their eligibility than others. Although there are some slight differences, the evidence suggests that doubts about eligibility occur in quite high proportions among both HB and SB non-claimants and are certainly not concentrated in any group (table 5.4).

Table 5.4 Doubts about eligibility by benefit group and characteristics of the claim unit

Proportions expressing doubts about eligibility

Benefit group		Composition of claim unit		Activity status	
		Non pensioners			
HB	48%	with no dependent children	53%	Working full or part time	53%
SB	55%	with dependent children	50%	Unemployed	(4/7)
FIS		**Pensioners**		Retired	41%
		Single person	35%	Other not working	(10/16)
		Married couple	59%		

The nature of people's doubts about eligibility take two rather different forms. On the one hand, there is a group of non-claimants who hold genuine misconceptions about the criteria for entitlement. A second group, however are much more vague about why they are not entitled and it is more a feeling of they *could not be* rather than that they *are not* eligible. This would suggest that other factors have an effect on perceptions of eligibility. It is useful to look in a little more detail at these two groups.

Misconceptions about eligibility criteria

Around 40% of the non-claimants who expressed some doubts about their eligibility appeared to have a genuine misconception about the criteria for entitlement. These varied between benefits but some of the more common concerned being in full or part time employment (for HB and SB), having savings (for HB), the effects of home ownership, (all benefits) and the receipt of another benefit, particularly unemployment benefit. The following two cases provide examples.

> Mr Shah is aged 43, and is married with three children. He is eligible for housing benefit. Although his command of English was not good, he had heard of housing benefit but thought it was only for unemployed people: 'Well as far as I have heard it is for people who don't work. People who are old can claim for it too... we never thought about it (benefits). The only benefit we know is child benefit nothing else; as I am working'.

> 'Well like I said when you are unemployed you just get unemployment benefit. The only other thing I have heard you can get when you are unemployed is rent rebate... But I'm not sure'
> (63 year old married man made redundant through ill health)

> 'Well I am not confident because I don't know if I'm going to be entitled to get this "FIS" or not. I might get it because I'm single, but not because I get a weekly wage.'
> (Single parent, aged 21)

The present research did not systematically investigate what misconceptions were held, or where they had come from, although other studies have done so before.[1] While these misconceptions draw attention to the need for clearly presented, and widely distributed, information about benefits, they do not entirely explain why a claim has been withheld. Most of those who held misconceptions were not very certain about the facts and in theory there was nothing to stop them going along to a benefit office to find out more. Some non-claimants, however, are very reluctant to go and ask until they are sure they are entitled.

> 'I've heard of people going and asking and being refused and so it's put me off. The fact of not liking going and being refused. I would hate myself really. I'd rather do anything, or mostly anything, than go to one of those offices and ask for help.'

It seems that uncertainty about entitlement is a powerful inhibitor, not just to making a claim, but even to making further enquiries. In other words, it can be used as a kind of 'excuse' for avoiding any contact with the benefit system. This would suggest that even where misconceptions are held, there are likely to be other negative forces at work.

The interactive effect of other factors

It is evident above that doubts about eligibility often cover much more deeply held attitudes towards claiming. Some people do not want to see themselves as eligible, others choose to avoid finding out because of their negative feelings towards claiming benefits or receiving income support. This was explicitly stated by one of the respondents in the study.

---

(1) See for example Corden, Ritchie and Matthews.

Mr Williams is a 60-year-old married man who is employed full time as a post office sorter. His wife, who was interviewed, had been trying to persuade him to apply for HB for some time, but he was resistant... 'He isn't interested.' He said, 'You won't get it.' I said, 'Well, why not?' He says, 'Because I am earning too much money.' But in her view his lack of willingness to try was partly an excuse to cover up his negative feelings about claiming benefits. She says that he views benefits as 'charity' and would not want his colleagues at work to think he could not manage and needed help.

A similar problem comes from views held about what kinds of people can get benefit. It is not uncommon to find that people will choose to exclude themselves from the benefit reference group and thus firmly believe they would be ineligible. The case below is illustrative:

Mrs Todd is a pensioner but she had not heard of HB before receiving the letter prior to the follow-up interview. However in her view it was not intended for people like her. 'It is for people on low incomes, hard-hit people like the unemployed living on social security. Everyone at rock bottom. Not so much pensioners who have furniture but people unemployed and still having to buy things for their homes.'

There are a range of other factors that can compound, or even manifest themselves as, doubts about eligibility. These include previous 'bad' experiences of claiming, either personal or reported and beliefs about what a claim will involve. These are factors we shall consider in subsequent sections of this chapter. It is clear from the preceding discussion, however, that uncertainty about entitlement is not simply an informational problem. Even when information about entitlement is given on a personalised basis, some people will choose to ignore it, or disbelieve it, because of other feelings or attitudes.

Before we leave this group who had doubts about their eligibility, it is useful to add a postscript about their subsequent claiming behaviour. It will be remembered that after the follow up interview, where these uncertainties about eligibility were expressed, we obtain information about any subsequent claims. It was found that 9% of the group who had some doubts eventually made a claim. Although this is a much lower figure than for people who thought they would be eligible (32%), it does suggest that some people will overcome their uncertainties and make a claim. We cannot, of course, tell whether this is because they had a misconception removed, they had a change of circumstance or whether the second interview in itself helped to reassure them about their entitlement.

Perceived utility

It is useful to consider here the effect of the perceived utility of the benefit on claiming behaviour. As we noted earlier, the measurement of this was in part reliant on peoples expectations of how much benefit they would receive which has some connection with knowledge and information about the benefit system. Although, a lack of perceived utility accounted for only a small proportion of predicted non-claimants, this could be simply a result of its location in the model (ie the 4th threshold).

Looking at the whole group of non-claimants it appears that a lack of perceived utility is not a very significant factor in preventing claims. Only 13% of all non-claimants thought the amount they would get was below the level they thought worth claiming while two thirds thought it would be more (ie they did perceive some utility). There was however a lot of uncertainty surrounding these answers and a sizeable group (21%) said they had no idea at all how much they would get. Although there must come a point in the general 'trade off' where the amount of potential entitlement outweighs other factors in a positive way, we suspect that it much more rarely acts negatively. It might of course do so if people were quite sure that there was only a very small amount involved. However given the complexities of benefit assessments, this information is quite difficult to ascertain unless a claim has been initiated or perhaps the advice of a welfare rights advisor sought.

5.3 Beliefs and feelings about the claim process

The Kerr model showed the negative beliefs and feelings about the claim process was an important threshold for predicting non-claimants. However, because it was the fifth threshold to be met, the model itself cannot show the size of the problem. We find, in fact, that using the measure developed for the model, over one third of the non-claimants (38%) had an overall negative view of the claim procedure. However 60% of them had already been lost to a claim at one of the earlier thresholds.

As was described earlier, the item used to measure beliefs and feelings for the model was a summed score across a number of different aspects of the claiming procedure. The aspects included were those about which people had the strongest views, and these are the features of the claim process that we shall consider in this section.

Table 5.5 shows the features of the claim process that were included in the model item, with the proportions of non-claimants holding negative beliefs about that aspect. Two points about the figures are notable. First, it seems to be the most public aspects of the claim procedure (eg applying to the benefit office, treatment by benefit officials, being in the company of other

Table 5.5 Non-claimants perceptions of the claim procedure: proportions holding negative views by benefit group

Aspects of claim procedure	HB	SB	FIS	Total
Proportions holding				
negative views about				
Applying to the benefit office	23%	39%	—	27%
Treatment by benefit officials	30%	39%	(1)	33%
Being in the company of other claimants	29%	46%	(1)	34%
Filling in a claim form	25%	13%	(+)	23%
Giving information about income	13%	10%	—	12%
Providing evidence for verification	10%	9%	(1)	11%
Average score:				
positive	3%	7%	(0)	4%
neutral	65%	42%	(4)	59%
negative	32%	50%	(1)	38%
Base:				
weighted	124	54	5	183
unweighted	65	49	5	119

claimants) which are most frequently negatively viewed by non-claimants. Second, perceptions about the SB claim procedure are, in general, more negative than for the HB procedure, but largely because of the aspects concerning contact with the social security office.

It has to be remembered that the non-claimants were describing their beliefs about the claim process. Although some of them may have had previous experience of claiming, most were describing what they *think* they would dislike about the process. It is therefore useful to consider how the views of the claimants, who had been through the process, compare with those of the non-claimants.

Table 5.6 compares the views of claimants and non-claimants for HB and SB. Judging by the overall score, it would seem that the feelings of those who have been though the process are not markedly different from those who are anticipating the procedure. Although overall, there are more negative views amongst non-claimants, the order of magnitude is not greatly significant. There is however some evidence to suggest that certain aspects of the claim procedure (eg filling in claim forms, giving information about income) cause more negative feelings in reality than they do in anticipation, while for other aspects (eg treatment by benefit officials) the situation is the reverse. In the main, this is true for both HB and SB, although a relatively high proportion of the HB claimants who had visited the office held quite negative views about the company of other claimants.

Table 5.6 Comparison of claimants and non-claimants perceptions of the claim procedure: proportions holding negative views by benefit group

Aspects of claim procedure	HB		SB	
	Claimant	Non-claimant	Claimant	Non-claimant
Proportions holding negative views about				
Applying to the benefit office	24%	23%	39%	39%
Visiting the benefit office	15%	N/A	31%	N/A
Treatment by benefit officials	21%	30%	23%	39%
Being in the company of other claimants	37%	29%	15%	46%
Filling in a claim form	28%	25%	31%	13%
Giving information about income	22%	13%	15%	10%
Providing evidence for verification	14%	10%	19%	9%
Average score:				
negative	28%	32%	32%	50%
neutral	67%	65%	67%	42%
positive	5%	3%	—	7%
Base:				
weighted	68	124	27	54
unweighted	32	65	28	49

Before we move on to consider how negative feelings about the claim procedure arise, we should note certain differences between claimant groups in their perceptions of what is involved. Three groups seem to hold particularly negative beliefs about the claim process. They are single pensioners (44%), pensioner couples (42%) and single person non-pensioners (53%). In fact, the evidence suggests that the problem is more related to age than to the composition of the claim unit. That is, it is those approaching retirement age and pensioners themselves who are more likely to hold negative views about the claiming procedure than other age groups.

Contact with the benefit office

Although HB and many SB claims can be made by post, it is quite usual to find that some visit to the benefit office has occurred during the claim process. Similarly for FIS claims, which are all made by post to Blackpool, visits to the local social security office are not uncommon.

As we have seen for non-claimants, the anticipation of these visits to the local office are quite negatively viewed, particularly by supplementary benefit claimants. In some cases this was connected with the physical location of the office, or the conditions that prevailed there. More often, however, an antipathy towards going to the office was connected with the image of the other people that may be there. In some cases this arose from a reluctance to mix with 'such' people, in others from a fear of identification with them.

> 'I'd never line up in that place. I'd never line up for anything. I'd never lower myself that much. I've seen them in _____ Street, when I go there. I see those poor blokes and women lining up. I don't want to get involved in all that. No way do I want to lower myself going down there.'
>
> (HB non-claimant)

> 'No thank you. Dirty, filthy lot down there. People tell me they break windows if they don't get what they want.'
>
> (SB non-claimant)

Another aspect of visiting benefit offices is the contact with benefit officials. Although this received some very strong adverse comment, it should be considered in the light of two facts. First, negative views must be balanced against a majority who either had no strong feelings or more positively thought that benefit officials did their best in a difficult environment. Secondly, benefit officials are now working under great pressure due to the increased number of claimants, staff cutbacks and changes in benefit administration (eg HB). In addition, some people are very sensitive when they make a claim, having overcome many inhibitions to do so.

Having said this, it is clear that some claimants feel that benefit officials have acted insensitively and simply being offhand can cause offence. An example of a comment about past treatment by benefit officials was as follows:

> 'I mean this is how the lady sat opposite me in the room. She said: "Do you think we are going to keep you and your child and that... and you are going to live on us." I mean that lady wasn't giving us anything out of her own pocket. It was her attitude. And she wasn't on her own, there were at least two more, but she was the worst.'
>
> (32-year-old, single parent)

Table 5.7 shows how different groups of non-claimants viewed the two aspects of visiting benefit offices discussed above. It can be seen that it is pensioner couples who are most worried about *both* aspects. Additionally, however, we see that pensioners are perhaps generally more worried about their exposure to other claimants than the treatment they will get from benefit officials.

Table 5.7 Proportions holding negative views about treatment by benefit officials and other claimants, by composition of the claim units

Proportions holding negative views about	Non-pensioners		Pensioners	
	Single person or lone parent(1)	Two parent families and married couples(2)	Single person	Married couple
Treatment by benefit officials	34%	37%	19%	42%
Company of other claimants	19%	33%	44%	47%
Base: All non-claimants				
weighted	47	57	46	33
unweighted	28	35	31	25

(1) includes 41 cases with no dependent children and 6 with dependent children
(2) includes 38 two parent families and 19 married couples without dependent children

How bad images of benefit offices are formed

There is no doubt that a previously bad experience at a benefit office has a strong negative impact. It can be enough to deter people claiming ever again, even in circumstances of high perceived need. It has been shown elsewhere that many people move in and out of eligibility for benefits and have intermittent contact with the benefit system over several years. Some of the non-claimants therefore referred back to previous experiences.

Being 'turned down' for a benefit is perhaps the most offputting experience. So humiliating is it for some people that it can stay with them for years. One of the reasons this may be so is that people have gone through the difficult process of declaring themselves to be in need. When they are then told by a benefit official that they are not 'in need', they feel, or even, are made to feel, that they are 'scrounging'. An example is provided by an elderly woman of 75 years who had been encouraged to claim by a hospital social worker after a visit to hospital:

> 'A social security officer came and visited and I mentioned I had some saving certificates. He just said: "Right! That's it! There is nothing we can do." and walked out. After that, I decided to forget the whole lot. I felt terrible. It seemed as if I was asking for charity.'

However, more often it was simply a bad personal contact at the office which was found to be 'degrading' and 'dehumanising'. Such an experience is vividly conjured up in the words of a 63 year old previous claimant of SB. She had a part-time job as a cleaner, and lived with her invalid retired sister. She described her experiences at the local security office.

> 'Well we sat there for two or three hours, didn't we? And when we got to the window, when we was called we was given about two minutes... I goes up and says to the woman:
> "I want to know about this form."
> "You haven't filled it in." she says.
> "I know. I wanted to ask you about it."
> "We haven't got time for that." she says... "Take it away and fill it in and bring it back."
> I just got up and walked away. I was disgusted. We sat there for two hours for that!'

She contrasted this with the help she had received at the CAB before finally making a successful claim. But she would not return to the office again. She disliked the office itself, the other claimants, the lack of privacy, but mostly what she felt to be the attitude of the staff who had dealt with her claim.

> 'Round this way you're made to feel degraded. You go there to ask for something, that's charity. Even though they say you're entitled to this and that benefit, that's the way it's given to you—as though it's charity.'

Some people, who have not had any contact with benefit offices, are deterred by the stories they hear. In some cases these may be told by friends or relatives; in others from accounts they see in the press. Certainly in the past, many popular newspapers have portrayed a very poor image of claimants with stories of 'scroungers' abounding. Even more factual reporting, as occurred in Hackney around the time of the introduction of Housing Benefit, can have its adverse effects. Several respondents referred to this and some acknowledged it had affected their decision to claim.

Providing information and evidence

It was noted earlier that certain aspects of the claim procedure are more negatively viewed by claimants than by those who are anticipating a claim. There were, however, particular groups of non-claimants, notably the elderly and those in employment, who expressed negative feelings about questions on income, earnings and savings. These ranged from a specific anxiety among the elderly about the amount of savings they had got, to a more general dislike of invasion of privacy. An example of the former is provided by a 61 year old man, in full-time employment, with a non-working wife and grown up children. He felt he was being penalised for 'good housekeeping' during his working life, by questions on savings.

> 'Savings—I feel that is a personal question and I can't see that it has anything to do with other people. What you've worked for all your life, that's your own private business.'

On the other hand, an employed woman of 57, in full-time employment, with a 15 year old son at school, was put off claiming HB by the fact her employer would have to sign the form:

> 'They want to know too much. They want you to take the form into work for your employer to sign it. That's embarrassing. If they ask for a pay slip, I think that should be adequate.'

When asked if she would be likely to claim in the near future, she replied:

> 'I probably will claim, but I'm not certain. I don't want my employer to sign the HB form so I will probably wait until I retire.'

However, for a 47 year old woman eligible for HB, in part-time work with a full-time employed husband, it was simply the idea of being asked personal questions which put her off.

> 'I don't like the idea of them asking you all those questions. What you earn is your own business, it turns you off filling in the form.'

The effort of claiming

One general factor that constantly emerges in any discussions of claiming is whether it is worth the effort. It is here that a potential claimant is truly involved in a process of trade off. On the one hand there is the prospect of some additional income; on the other there is the time and effort involved in making a claim with all the negative connotations that may hold. In this respect, people who are working seem particularly prone to a negative outcome. Firstly, they are more doubtful about whether there is going to be any real benefit in making a claim; second, they have to find the time, during working hours, to deal with the claim procedure. For these reasons, the prospect of any complexity, or time-consuming queuing, is likely to act as a deterrent.

5.4 Unstable circumstances

The final threshold in the model concerns the individuals' perceptions of the stability of their circumstances. The hypothesis is that if people see their circumstances as unstable they may use this as a reason for delaying or even avoiding a claim. Although, a perception of unstable circumstances was not numerically large in predicting non-claimants in the model, it was, as with the other later thresholds, much more widespread among non-claimants as a whole. One quarter of the non-claimants either thought their financial circumstances were likely to improve in the next few months or mentioned some forthcoming change in circumstance which affected their decision to claim. As is already evident, however, a very high proportion (89%) of this group had already been predicted as non-claimants because of one of the earlier thresholds. This would suggest that the rationale of delaying a claim because of possibly changing circumstances is very commonly accompanied by other factors which inhibit claims.

5.5 Attitudes towards income support

We have already suggested that negative attitudes towards being in receipt of benefits permeate virtually all elements of the decision to claim. There is however a problem in measuring such attitudes since they are often implicit rather than explicit in what is being said. (Many of the verbatim answers quoted in this chapter serve to illustrate this point.) It was for this reason that we made no attempt in this study to question the stigmatising aspects of benefit claims. We had no confidence we would succeed with the structured form of interview being used.

In any discussion of take-up, however, it is vital to understand the processes that are at work. There are two main reasons for this. First, much previous research has shown that negative feelings about benefit support are shared almost equally by claimants and non-claimants. In other words, they can be and are overcome, when other forces are dominant. Second, it is likely that any reduction in these negative attitudes would be the single most useful contributer to increasing take up, since such attitudes underly everything else.

Behind the negative feelings which inhibit decisions to claim are some fundamental values of our society. Indeed, so fundamental are they that people find it difficult to explain quite why they are so vital. Perhaps the most salient in understanding take up is the importance of 'independence'. This is variously described as being 'proud', not wanting 'charity', 'standing on your own feet' but always comes back to an antipathy towards 'dependence'.

Such attitudes have a powerful effect on people's perceptions of what the claim process will involve. The fact that many of the resistant non-claimants negatively anticipate their treatment by benefit officials or their exposure to other claimants is as much to do with underlying attitudes as it is to do with reality. However these negative attitudes have a more pervasive effect—they make people want to manage, at all costs, so that they can avoid perceiving a need to claim; they lead people to believe they would not be eligible, because they do not want to be eligible and so on.

As we have said, this research can add nothing new to an understanding of these underlying attitudes, but, this has already been done effectively by previous research. What this study has done is to confirm that negative attitudes towards to the very notion of income support are embedded in so many explanations of non-claiming.

5.6 Summary and conclusions

This chapter has explored the nature of the forces working within the Kerr model, and in particular the factors which inhibit movement across the thresholds. It has shown that of the six variables contained within the model, a lack of perceived need, uncertainty about eligibility and negative beliefs and feelings about the claim process are by far the most important. Examination of individual examples has shown that there is often more then one inhibiting factor involved and the interrelationship between the most powerful inhibitors has been demonstrated. This may indicate that movement across one threshold may be associated with movement across others but this has not been systematically investigated. It is suggested that underpinning many of the negative factors is a strongly negative attitude towards the concept of income support or benefit receipt.

The positive forces: factors which encourage claiming

6.1 Introduction

We turn now to consider the factors which encourage people to claim means tested benefits. In relation to the Kerr model, these can be seen as the forces which help to move people across thresholds and thus tip the decision to claim in a positive direction.

In this chapter we shall be turning the focus on to the group who had become claimants by the time of the follow up interview. They are a group of particular interest since they had undergone the conversion from eligible non-claimants (in the Autumn of 1983) to claimants (in the Summer of 1984). As in the last chapter, however, we will occasionally compare their views or experiences with people who were still non-claimants, to look for the differences or similarities.

As a starting point, it is useful to consider the influences that the newly converted claimants mentioned as having led them towards a claim. Three precipitating factors were spontaneously mentioned with some frequency:

- They had had a change of circumstances which increased their need to claim benefits. (43%)

- There had been a specific event, such as the arrival of a gas bill, an increase in rent, which had precipitated some action. (28%)

- They had been advised or encouraged to claim by another person. (47%)

In the context of the Kerr model, two particular thresholds, perceived need and perceived eligibility, were directly affected by these stated influences. It is with these that we shall begin a discussion of the positive forces.

6.2 Increased awareness of need

A change of circumstance In some instances the need for additional income arises directly from a major change in circumstances. Becoming unemployed is perhaps the most obvious, but retirement, becoming widowed, moving house, having children etc, may also lead to changes in levels of need. At such times, an eligible non-claimant is likely to be more receptive to the advantages of claiming, however much they may want to avoid it.

A change of circumstance appears to have been particularly important to the new SB claimants. Two thirds of those who subsequently claimed SB mentioned such a change amongst their reasons for claiming, compared with a third of those who claimed HB. Although on the surface this may appear to be an obvious finding, it has to be remembered that all of these people were assessed as eligible for SB *prior* to the change of circumstance to which they are referring. Part of the answer, of course, lies with the unemployed claimants who started to claim SB when their period of unemployment benefit came to an end. For the other claimants, however, and particularly the pensioners, it was a circumstance, *in addition* to the one that had already made them eligible for SB, that led them to claim.

Although a change of circumstance was often given as the start of the decision to claim, there were a number of cases where some delay had occured before the actual claim was made. The following examples are cases in point:

> 'He didn't want to do it, but I was beginning to feel pressured. My husband doesn't really like claiming for anything. I get paid once a month but it's really not much. Having to pay the rates and rent, my wages weren't enough to pay all the bills... He didn't like it, knowing my husband, he doesn't like begging. When he became unemployed it took him a long time to go and claim his money (SB). If he could do without, he would. He asked because of the bills. He didn't like it at all. He found it degrading.'
>
> (Wife, employed full-time; husband (26), unemployed)

> 'My husband always intended to apply (for HB) when he was alive. When I was going through his papers after he died I found the form so I decided to apply... (The survey interview) sort of confirmed the fact. I'd already made up my mind, but it gave me a push. When I had this visit it sort of made up my mind.
>
> (63-year-old widow)

Events It was common to find that a single event had frequently acted as a trigger to a claim, particularly for the HB claimants. In almost all cases, it was an event that brought the non-claimant face to face with the difficulties they were having in managing financially. The 'event' concerned may have been the arrival of a bill, an increase in rent, a rates demand, the need to buy some large household item or even a sudden realisation of how much debt had accumulated. Whatever the cause, a perception of being in need quite suddenly emerged. Again, however, there may have been some delay in making a claim, although usually not very prolonged.

It is important to note here that there were some people who were still non-claimants who had had similar events or changes of circumstance. In other words they too were 'delaying' a claim but they were on the other side of the claim threshold. So although changes or events can be a precipitating factor, they will not necessarily be so if the balance of negative forces is greater.

6.3 Personalised information, advice and encouragement

The remainder of this chapter will be devoted to considering the impact of personal information, advice and encouragement on the decision to claim. The fact that we are giving this topic so much weight is not simply reflective of its evident importance to people who converted to claimants. As we hope to show, an encouragement to claim benefits is one of the most important influences on the claim decision not least because it has a bearing on all the major inhibiting forces. In other words it is a major factor in helping non-claimants to cross the threshold towards a claim.

Information We have already discussed the fact that simply having information about benefits is not sufficient to precipitate or encourage a claim. Furthermore, there is now accumulated research evidence which shows that intensive publicity about benefits has only a marginal effect on take up.[1] Table 6.1, which shows the proportions of claimants and non-claimants who had seen information or publicity about the benefit for which they were eligible, therefore confirms what is already known. It is worth noting, however, that the proportion of people who had seen information and publicity was higher among the HB group than the SB (or FIS) group.

Table 6.1 Sources of publicity and information about main benefits, by claim action and benefit group

Benefit information	Claim action		Benefit for which eligible		
	Claimant	Non-Claimant	HB	SB	FIS
Had seen information or publicity about the benefit (before claim)	72%	78%	80%	62%	60%
Sources of information					
Poster or notice	39%	42%	43%	30%	30%
Leaflets	33%	31%	35%	23%	20%
Radio or TV	16%	42%	36%	35%	20%
Newspapers, or magazines	9%	36%	32%	22%	30%
GLC information[1]	17%	20%	23%	19%	10%
Other	39%	17%	23%	17%	10%
Base: All respondents:					
Weighted	99	183	92	81	9
Unweighted	65	119	97	77	10

[1] The GLC Welfare Rights Campaign was active in Hackney just after the first interview for the Hackney Benefit Study.

Although we know information in itself will not precipitate a claim, it can be one among a number of influences. One third of the claimants said that information they had seen had had some bearing on their decision to claim and around half of this number said it had had a significant influence. The importance of information being comprehensible, relevant and timely, therefore, needs to be stressed. In recent years considerable strides have been made in the presentation of information about benefits, both from within the DHSS itself, and by welfare rights groups. It is not an easy task to make the benefit system comprehensible, but many new documents have gone a long way towards doing so. It is equally important however that the information should be available at the appropriate time. For this reason the practice of sending out leaflets about benefits with notifications of rent increases, fuel bills, when people move (as is operated by some housing associations), when claims for national insurance benefits are made etc, are to be applauded. In addition, there is some new research evidence which suggests that the more

(1) The most recent evidence for this comes from the evaluation of the GLC Welfare Rights Campaign.

personalised, accessible and retrievable the information is, the greater the likelihood of its being used.[1]

Advice and encouragement   We have already noted that about half of the claimants mentioned personalised advice or encouragement as one of the factors that had led to a claim. The sources of influence mentioned by this group were one or more of the following:

- DHSS or local authority benefit officers (8%)
- Welfare rights workers (6%)
- Officials such as housing officers, social workers, doctors, solicitors etc (15%)
- Personal friends, relatives, neighbours, colleagues etc (22%)
- SCPR, through participation in the study (29%)

As might be expected, participation in the study had an influence on some of the people who decided to claim. Although it was rarely the only influence mentioned, a number of the claimants referred to the first interview, or the letter informing about eligibility, as having helped in their decision to claim.

It is evident that, as with written information, advice or encouragement needs to come at the right time. This is well illustrated by the following answers about why a claim had been made.

'By the time your (SCPR) letter (about possible eligibility) came, my circumstances had changed completely so I had to claim. I was out of work and getting into debt. It takes you a long time to get out of debt when you've been in it. I couldn't pay my maintenance payments. Now I'm on SB and having my maintenance paid directly.'

(26 year old man, SB claimant)

'When I first moved they gave us lots of leaflets to read... I went down to the CAB office to talk to them. I was already drawing (HB) but the man told me I was entitled to more benefit and I put in an application.'

(27 year old man with wife and two children)

'The enormous amount of the rates. I'd never expected so much as they sent me a bill for (£1,340). What I'd expected I'd have been more amenable to pay... I was out of work and (partner) was on low money... (Her mother) said are you claiming all you should... And it was your lady (SCPR interviewer) that helped...'

(35 year old woman on HB)

As is apparent from these cases, advice or encouragement to claim will often be very effective if it comes at a time when non-claimants are experiencing some kind of change or difficult circumstance. If, for example, an awareness of need is emerging, then personal advice towards a claim will fall on fertile ground.

Another way in which advice can have an important effect on a decision to claim is by heightening a person's awareness of their own need. Such advice can provide the non-claimant with a legitimacy to claim which again may overcome other doubts about a claim.

---

[1] Hedges and Ritchie 1988.

It is important to note that some of the people who remained non-claimants throughout the study had also been advised or encouraged to claim, and not least, through participation in the research. However, the number who spontaneously mentioned such advice as having had any effect on their thinking about a claim was almost insignificant (13%). However, as we have discussed at length, many of the non-claimants had overridden the advice they had been given with strong doubts about their own eligibility.

Social approval It has already been noted that a sizeable proportion of the claimants had been encouraged to claim the benefit by a friend, relative, neighbour, colleague etc. Such encouragement can not only overcome any uncertainty about making the claim but also helps to make the state of being a claimant acceptable.

During the course of the interview, all the respondents were asked about the attitudes of close relatives or friends, towards their claiming benefit. The primary concern was with people whose views were of importance to the respondent, and who might therefore influence their actions. Table 6.2 shows the picture that emerged. Three points are notable from this. First, it seems that social approval is by no means essential to a claim, but overall it has some positive effect. Second, the level of approval for claiming housing benefit seems to be generally higher than the approval for claiming supplementary benefit. Third, and this is an initially puzzling finding, whether or not other people approve seems to have little bearing on claims for SB. This becomes less puzzling when we bring two pieces of information together. It can be seen from table 6.2 that pensioners are apparently less influenced by the approval of friends or relatives than those under pensionable age. We also showed earlier that a high proportion of the SB non-claimants are pensioners. Unfortunately the numbers are too small to analyse by benefit type and claim unit composition but this is likely to explain why social approval appears to have less effect on claims for SB. What it also suggests however is that, for groups such as pensioners, who have been shown to hold negative feelings about the claim process, approval from an informal source

Table 6.2 Social approval for a claim, by claim action taken and benefit group and characteristics of the claim unit

Benefit group and characteristics of claim unit	Proportions who had some approval to claim which mattered		Total
	claimants	non-claimants	
Housing Benefit	74%	56%	63%
Supplementary Benefit	37%	50%	46%
All benefits	65%	54%	58%
Non-pensioners			
With dependent children	74%	59%	63%
With no dependent children	67%	50%	57%
Pensioners			
Single person	} 52%	51%	48%
Married couple		63%	64%

may be less powerful in overcoming all the doubts and uncertainties about making a claim.

6.4 Changing attitudes towards the benefit system: the interactive effect of positive influences

We have already seen that negative feelings about the claim process or about the idea of receiving benefits can be a major deterrent to a claim. Such feelings however are the most difficult deterrents to remove since they are constantly reinforced. This reinforcement comes from the benefit system itself, from reported experiences, from media coverage and even perhaps from societal attitudes towards the importance of independence. There is however evidence to suggest that positive influences of the type described in this chapter can begin to overcome negative attitudes, particularly amongst certain groups.

As support for this, we will draw on some additional analysis undertaken during the course of this study, using GLIM (a statistical package for the fitting of Generalised Linear Models). The opportunity[1] to undertake this analysis arose after the study had been designed and, in this respect, its scope was limited. Nevertheless, it provided an opportunity to test certain hypotheses about claiming behaviour, even if only in a preliminary way.

A full account of the analysis undertaken, together with relevant technical details of GLIM, are given in Appendix II. In outline, the aim is to identify the variables, and interactions between variables, which have a significant effect on claiming behaviour. This is done through the model fitting procedures available within GLIM. Simply put, these provide an extension of the familiar test, which may be used to determine whether a single variable is or is not associated with claiming behaviour, to the multivariate situation where the relationship between a group of two or more variables and claiming behaviour may be examined simultaneously.[2]

Although limitations were imposed on the use of the method, both by the specific measurement of the variables (because they were not designed for the purpose) and by the size of the sample to which GLIM was applied, the results suggest some preliminary conclusions which cannot be ignored in the context of this report. These are reported below, with all the cautions noted in the full appendix.

Ten variables were used in the GLIM analysis.[3] These were
Perceived need
Perceived eligibility
Encouragement to claim
Perceived social acceptability of claiming
Attitudes towards benefit support (whether there are stigmatising effects of claiming)

---

(1) The opportunity arose through the involvement of Jennifer Waterton, a statistician in SCPR's Methods Centre. She is the author of the technical appendix on the use of GLIM.

(2) Such methods have been available for quantitative data (through the use of regression analysis, analysis of variance etc) for many years but the application to categorical data has only been developed in the last 10 years.

(3) The measurement of these variables was not the same as for the rest of the Kerr model, because the items had to be drawn from the first Hackney Benefit Study (see Appendix II).

Beliefs and feelings about the claiming procedure
Gender and partnership
Whether has dependent children
Age of the head of the claim unit
Employment status of the head of the claim unit.

The outcome variable was whether or not a claim had been made by the time of the record check. The analysis was applied to *all* the 184 respondents involved in the study, who were all non-claimants at the time of the main Hackney Benefit Study.

The analysis undertaken provides some important findings:

- the existence of some encouragement to claim, whether from formal or informal sources is of critical importance in the decision to claim.

- Age, perceived need, and social acceptability (together with an encouragement to claim) are in a top league of factors which discriminate claimants from non-claimants.

- Perceived eligibility, though less important than the items mentioned above, does discriminate significantly between claimants and non-claimants.

- Although less strong than the individual effects there is an interactive effect between an encouragement to claim *and* beliefs and feelings about the claim process, perceived eligibility and the age of the potential claimant.

- There is some evidence of an interactive effect between beliefs and feelings about the claim process and attitudes towards benefit support.

There are three important implications of these findings. First, they provide added support to the evidence which has been yielded through the Kerr model. That is, they confirm that perceived need and perceived eligibility are important elements in the decision to claim.[1] Second, they tell us of other factors, not included in the Kerr model, which have a significant effect on the decision to claim. By far the most important of these is some personal encouragement to claim the benefit concerned. Thirdly, the interactive effect of an encouragement to claim with other factors shows where it can be particularly effective. That is, it has the greatest effect on the claiming behaviour of older people; it is most likely to precipitate a claim among people who are uncertain about their eligibility; and that it can have a significant effect on the claiming behaviour of those who have negative feelings about the claim process.

None of these findings came as a surprise. Indeed, many of the conclusions are not new to take up research. However, what the analysis has done is to provide strong confirmation of the important influences on take up across three different benefit groups and amongst a large number of non-claimants. Again, this was a prospective analysis in the sense that the data used for the

---

(1) Although the GLIM analysis does not appear to confirm the importance of beliefs and feelings about the claim process, this is almost certainly a result of the measure which had to be used (see Appendix II).

GLIM model was drawn from views and experiences held *prior* to any benefit claim.

Clearly the choice of the original 10 variables for inclusion is crucial. We cannot rule out that some other variable which we have not measured, or one we have measured in an unsatisfactory fashion, would provide a more significant account of claiming behaviour. Although we do have some reservations about one or two of the measures, we believe that the crucial factors affecting claiming behaviour have been included.

Taking the analysis a stage further, it is possible to tentatively propose a model of variables, and interactions between variables, which would have sufficient terms to account for differences between claimants and non-claimants. It is as follows:

Claiming behaviour is determined by:
An encouragement to claim
Perceived need; Age; Social acceptability of claiming;
Perceived eligibility; Attitudes towards benefit support;
Beliefs and feelings about the claim process

AND interactions between
Age x attitudes towards benefit support;
Beliefs and feelings x attitudes towards benefit support;
Encouragement to claim x perceived eligibility
Encouragement to claim x perceived need
Encouragement to claim x age.

Another way of looking at this is to say that in order to predict the probability of claiming[1] for a given individual, we would need to have a measure of each of the individual variables shown and of key interactions between them. There is no way in which this model could be tested in this study because of the sample size. Indeed, it is difficult to envisage any take up study which could do so prospectively since the resources needed to find a sufficient number of eligible non-claimants would be very considerable indeed. However, in a sense, testing the model would be just a statistical and theoretical nicety. It is much more important that those involved in trying to increase take up feel some certainty about the major inhibitions to claim and even more crucial that we understand at least some of the factors that can help to overcome these negative forces. If nothing else, the model shows us the powerful effect of a personal encouragement to claim.

---

(1) The model proposed above would predict a probability of claiming. This is an important distinction from the threshold approach which only allows probabilities of 0 (no claim) or 1 (claim).

Summary and implications

In this final chapter we shall review the evidence provided by this research and consider its implications for the take up of income related benefits. We begin with a brief digest of the main findings and the conclusions to which these lead. We then move on to consider the relevance of these findings for the income related benefits introduced in April 1988. In the final part of this chapter we consider the implications of the research for some strategies to improve the take up of income related benefits.

7.1 Main Findings of the Research

There are a number of findings of this research which are of importance in understanding the issues surrounding the take up of means tested benefits. The following seem to be of most significance:

Changes in claiming behaviour

1. Over the two year period monitored by the study (ie Autumn '83 to June '85), 44% of the eligible non-claimants became claimants and 56% remained non-claimants. Certain groups were identified as being particularly claim resistant, most notably

    - people approaching or well over retirement age
    - two parent families
    - owner occupiers
    - people in full time employment.

    Most of these were groups which were shown to have particularly low take up rates in the Hackney Benefit Study.

The Kerr Threshold Model

2. The Kerr threshold model was shown to have a high success rate in predicting behaviour and particularly for cases which *failed* to claim. This would suggest that the six variables contained within the model, when negatively aspected, include more of the key inhibitions to a claim.

3. The model has a predictive power for both SB and HB, although it is much stronger for SB. However, for both benefits, the model's ability to predict non-claimants is high. This would suggest that the processes at work are not benefit specific and have some general application to those containing a means tested component.

The negative forces: factors which discourage claiming

4. Of the six elements contained within the threshold model, three are thought to be of particular importance in explaining non-claiming. These are a lack of perceived need, uncertainty about eligibility and negative beliefs and feelings about the claim process. Of the remaining three, the deterrent effect of unstable circumstances was found to be of greater significance than the others. An absence of knowledge about the benefit's existence was the least important of the six variables covered.

5. There is a clear interrelationship between the three most significant deterrents to claiming. That is, a lack of perceived need, uncertainty about eligibility and negatives attitudes towards the claiming process often co-exist. It is thought therefore that a change in any one of these elements might reduce the deterrent effect of others.

6. An examination of the nature and basis of the major inhibiting factors suggests that they are often underpinned by negative attitudes towards the whole concept of income support. It is suggested that any reduction in such attitudes would be the single most useful contributor to increasing take up since they permeate virtually all elements of the claim decision process.

The positive forces: factors which encourage take up

7. Two main factors were explicitly mentioned by claimants as being important in their decision to claim. These were:

    (1) a change of circumstance or an event which increased their awareness or level of 'need';

    (2) personal advice or encouragement to claim.

8. Some further statistical analysis (undertaken with the use of GLIM) suggests that the existance of some encouragement to claim, whether from formal or informal sources is of critical importance in the decision to claim. It is suggested that this is because it has an influence on underlying attitudes towards income support (by providing legitimacy and social approval for a claim) and this in turn has an effect on the major inhibiting factors identified in the Kerr model.

General conclusions

9. The research provides strong confirmation of the findings of much previous research. In particular, it confirms that:

    - there is no single cause of non-take up;
    - there are a number of inhibiting or delaying factors of which some are more powerful than others;
    - the inhibiting factors are complex and intricate, influenced by underlying attitudes towards the concept of income support.

10. It is argued that in order to increase take up, the positive influences have to be increased so that they outweigh the negative forces and hence help people to cross the necessary thresholds to a claim. An encouragement to claim, whether from formal or informal sources, is seen as a particularly powerful positive influence.

7.2 Implications for the new system of income related benefits

The new social security scheme introduced in 1988 provides three weekly paid income related benefits. These are:

Income Support which is available to people who are not in employment or full time education, and whose income does not exceed an 'applicable amount' (ie, an amount appropriate to the claimant and his or her family). In principle, although not entirely in detail, income support is a replacement for supplementary benefit.

Family Credit which is available to people in employment, who have dependent children and whose income does not exceed a particular level. This is a replacement for Family Income Supplement, although the administration of the benefit is different from the current system for FIS.

Housing Benefit which is available in respect of rent and rates to people whose income does not exceed the 'applicable amount' for the claimant and his or her household (or exceeds it only to an extent that is specified). In principle, although again not in detail, this is a continuation of the previous system of housing benefit.

All three benefits require a check of income or resources against 'needs' and they continue to involve a means test. There is therefore nothing about the new benefits that is likely to outdate the findings of this study. Indeed, all the processes involved in the claiming decision and all the issues surrounding take up which have been described have direct application to the new system.

7.3 Implications for promoting take up

Given the new system of income related benefits it is timely to consider how take up levels can be brought to their maximum level. Although it was not part of the brief for this research to consider promotional strategies, we cannot let the opportunity pass without drawing attention to the leads suggested by some of the key findings.

An encouragement to claim

Perhaps the most important finding of the research is the positive impact of personalised advice or encouragement on the decision to claim, particularly when it arises at the 'right time'. This information, however, does not immediately suggest any easy solutions since it implies that the potential claimant has already been identified by, or has been brought into contact with, some 'encouraging' source. The lack of easy solutions, however, should not mean that we ignore the finding completely. Indeed, we would argue that an encouragement to claim has to be both multi-faceted and sustained and that therefore all possible avenues should be explored. We would suggest that the following are approaches that would be helpful.

DHSS Publicity   There will need to be publicity about the new benefits. This will need to convey positive images of the benefits and of the groups they are intended for. It also seems important that, through imaginative advertising strategies, they should convey a message of 'encouragement to claim'.

Welfare Rights and Advice Centres   Welfare rights organisations, citizen's advice bureaux, law centres and other advice agencies already play an important part in helping and encouraging people to claim their full benefit entitlement. Any extension of their role, through either central or local government support, would therefore have a positive effect on the level of claims.

Advice from other professional and official sources

There is no doubt that the advice of a professional, or of an official in some other capacity, can be very effective in promoting claims. Some thought might therefore be given to how those who have contact with potential claimants, particularly in times of difficulty, might be given advice or informational support to help their client claim. Although social workers are already involved in such a way, there are many other groups, such as doctors, other health professionals, people working within the legal or penal system, community workers, housing officers etc who could provide the appropriate advice at the right time.

Informal networks   Many claimants, or potential claimants, hear about the benefit system through friends, neighbours, colleagues, and other informal networks. In addition, for reasons we have already discussed, some encouragement to claim from an informal contact can have positive effects. Perhaps therefore some consideration should be given to how such methods can be fully utilised. Running some form of campaign among claimants to 'Help a friend claim a benefit' might be one such example.

These are just some tentative suggestions as to how an encouragement to claim can be more wide spread. Some of them are clearly quite easy to introduce and there are undoubtedly others that could be suggested. Our main recomendation however is that the power of personal advice and encouragement should be fully utilised on as many fronts as is practical.

Increasing certainty about eligibility   We have discussed how uncertainty about entitlement is not simply a result of poor information about the benefit system. However this does not mean that clearly presented and well designed benefit literature is not important. The DHSS already has a Document Design Unit which has made some considerable advances in improving both the information content and the presentational style of many forms, leaflets, letters and other benefit documents. Such advances should be encouraged since they can have an effect on claiming in more than one way. First, by making benefit information easier to absorb, they will help to clarify how the system works and hopefully decrease the number of misconceptions. Secondly, they help to convey an image of the benefit system which is less 'down at heel' and which in turn helps to promote a more positive image of claimants. Research already undertaken for the Document Design Unit has produced some evidence to this effect.

Removing negative feelings about the claim process

We have seen that negative attitudes towards the claiming process can be a serious deterrent to a claim. In many cases, these negative attitudes are based on perceptions which may have come from hearsay or a media image or may be the result of much more deeply held feelings about the benefit system. For this group, who have no experience of the claim process, any of the suggestions already noted should help to overcome some of these negative beliefs.

But there are people who hold negative views who do so from the base of experience. It is all too easy to say that every claim should be handled with care, sensitivity and patience by benefit officials. Many claims are so handled, and where they are not, it is often a result of heavy workloads or even the heightened vulnerabilities of the claimants themselves that exacerbate the problem. Nevertheless any bad experience can have a deleterious effect on subsequent claiming behaviour. This is true not only for the person who may themselves have experienced the difficulty but also for people to whom that experience is reported. All we can say is that full awareness of the effects of these experiences is important.

Targetting the relevant groups

We have seen that some groups of potential claimants appear to be especially resistant to claiming. Of particular concern in this context are two parent families, where it is not just the claimant who is being deprived of income. In these cases, the children of the family are also being financially disadvantaged because of the resistance to claim by their parents. It is not within our expertise to suggest how groups such as two parent families, or any of the other resistors, might be targeted. However, the results of this research would suggest that there could be some benefit in doing so, either by specially designed publicity, or through some of the other means already referred to. Certainly, we have a feeling that if the 'need' to claim was legitimised for two parent families (ie, by drawing attention to the needs of the children) it might have quite a positive effect on claiming. A similar case, although differently targetted, could be made for the other groups of claim 'resistors'.

We have used this final chapter to discuss just a few ways in which the evidence from this research might be utilised. There are clearly other possibilities that could be suggested and further reflection on these is required. To conclude, however, we would wish to return to a very general finding from this research, but one which has a number of implications. That is, there are a number of countervailing forces surrounding the decision to claim. Only by increasing the positive and reducing the negative will the threshold to a claim be crossed.

Appendices

APPENDIX I Table of response rates by main benefit and sample type

APPENDIX II The use of GLIM by Jennifer Waterton

APPENDIX III Study documents

APPENDIX I Response rate by main benefit and sample type

Sample selection and response	Main benefit (main sample only) HB SB FIS	Sample Main	Supple-mentary	TOTAL	
Selected for interview	162 56 15	233	121	354	
Permission not given for second approach	10 1 —	11	8	19	
Issued for interview	152 55 15	222	113	335	
Died	1 1 —	2	—	2	
Moved, new address not known/traced	15 2 1	18	14	32	
TOTAL IN SCOPE for interview	136 52 14	202	99	301	= 100%
Full interview	97 28 10	135	49	184	61%
Interviewed but found ineligible for follow-up study*	1 7 1	9	19	28	9%
Refusal	23 8 —	31	16	47	16%
Non-contact	11 7 1	19	7	26	9%
Ill, in hospital, away during survey period	4 1 2	7	2	9	3%
Other reasons	— 1 —	1	6	7	2%

* These people were found to be claiming the relevant benefit at the time of the first interview. As can be seen the majority were from the supplementary sample for whom only screen interview information was available (see Chapter 2).

APPENDIX II The use of GLIM by Jennifer Waterton, SCPR Survey Methods Centre

Introduction

Much statistical analysis requires a facility for fitting *linear models* to observed distributions. One statistical package which has been developed for this task is GLIM (Generalised Linear Interactive Modelling, R J Baxter and J A Nelder, 1978). Although a similar kind of analysis can be done within SPSS-X, a package much more familiar to the social scientist, the SPSS-X does not have the flexibility nor ease of execution nor readability of GLIM. Additionally, some problems have been identified with the loglinear procedure which has only recently been added. Although GLIM can be put to a variety of purposes, the kernel of the package is the algorithm for the fitting of *generalised linear models*. This provides a unified framework embracing classical linear regression with normal errors, loglinear models for contingency tables, logit and probit models for the analysis of proportions, and models with gamma errors. Model specification is simple but powerful, allowing refinements such as prior weights and fixing of certain parameter values.

In the analysis conducted for the Hackney Benefit Study, the (discrete) dependent variable y_i is the number of individuals who claim benefit out of the total n_i individuals who have identical levels of each of the factors, considered, for the analysis being conducted, as the independent (or predicting) variables. Each of these n_i individuals is considered, in statistical language to be an independent 'trial' which can result in 'success' (ie the individual claims) or 'failure' (ie the individual does not claim). Each trial has a probability of success π_i which varies with i, the particular combination of factor levels. Then y_i is distributed as a binomial random variable with probability of success π_i and number of trials n_i. This may be written.

$$y_i = n_i \pi_i + \Sigma_i$$

where Σ_i represents binomial deviations from expectation. If the concomitant variables are continuous, then this is known as the probit model (Finney, 1952). When the concomitant variables are categorical, as in this case, we fit a logistic model (Cox, 1970). The logistic model uses the *logistic transform*, η_i, of the discrete counts (y_i) as the dependent variable. Thus,

$$\eta_i = \log \left[\frac{\frac{y_i}{n_i}}{1 - \frac{y_i}{n_i}} \right]$$

$$\eta_i = \log \left[\frac{y_i}{n_i - y_i} \right]$$

Thus, in all linear modelling there are three steps in defining the model—declaring the *dependent* variate (in this case the y_is), declaring the *error structure* (in this case Binomial) and declaring the *link function* (in this case the logistic transform). The next step is then to declare the model, or sequence of models to be fitted. The program will then estimate the relevant model parameters, using maximum likelihood procedures, and will calculate a measure of the goodness of fit of the model, called the *deviance* which has, asymptotically, the properties of the X^2 distribution. Thus it is possible to assess the effect of including or excluding particular terms from the model. This is because of the following result (Kendall and Stuart, 1967). If d_i is the deviance under model 1 and d_2 is the deviance under model 2 and if model 2 is nested in model 1 (ie the parameters estimated under model 2 are a subset of the parameters estimated under model 1) then d_1-d_2 is distributed as X^2 with degrees of freedom equal to the difference in the numbers of parameters estimated under the two models.

The search for the best fitting model entails a strategy whereby the most parsimonious model (ie the model with fewest parameters) which provides an adequate representation (in terms of the scaled deviance) is sought. This process allows the significance of all main effects of factors and inter-action effects between factors to be assessed. The best fitting model, once identified, may then be examined in more detail by scrutinising the parameter estimates themselves. In effect there will be one parameter for each level of each factor (main effect) and one parameter for each combination of factor levels for each 2-way and higher order interactions. There is some redundancy in the above parameterisation, so some parameters (for instance, the first level of each main effect) are automatically set to zero and provide the reference point for other levels of the factor. Thus a *positive* parameter estimate for a given level of any factor indicates there is an increased propensity to claim benefit associated with that factor level, while a *negative* parameter estimate implies the reverse. Similar conclusions may be drawn for 2-way and higher order interactions.

Given the limitations on size of the data set, it was impossible to model the y_is as functions of the 10 factors identified as potentially important simultaneously. This is because a requirement of the logistic model is that each cell as defined by the factors should be non-zero. With only 121 observations, a 10-way classification would result in large numbers of empty cells. Thus our approach was to look at factors in groups of 3, ensuring that all 2-way interactions were examined. The complete set of models for one of the seven analyses together with the deviances and the parameter estimates for the fitted model, are given below (see Table 1). For the remaining 6 analyses the fitted model only is given (see Tables 2–7).

It was planned that the GLIM analysis should be undertaken for people who were eligible non-claimants at the time of the main Hackney study. This made it possible to examine actual claiming behaviour against predicted claiming behaviour for the maximum number of people. Because of this, however, the variables had to be derived from information collected at the time of the main study, or from items which specially asked about experiences *prior to* a claim. This means that one or two of the items used are thought to be weak since they were simply the best proxy available for the measure required (eg BF).

The items used were chosen to contain a mix of demographic variables, threshold measures and factors thought to have a positive influence on the decision to claim. All of the variables contained dimensions which were thought to have a bearing on claiming behaviour. The 10 variables used were composited as follows:

Perceived need (PN)

Response to statement *You don't feel you need the money enough to make the claim.*

Agrees strongly	(1) No perceived need.
Agrees to some extent Can't say	(2) Possible perceived need
Does not agree at all	(3) Definite perceived need

Perceived eligibility (PE)

Thought might be eligible for SB, FIS or HB	(1) Perceived eligibility
Did not think eligible for SB, FIS or HB or did not know	(2) Does not know about eligibility

Beliefs and feelings (BF)

Response to statement *You don't like going to social security or other benefit offices.*

Agrees strongly	(1) Strongly negative feelings
Agrees to some extent	(2) Negative feelings
Can't say	(3) Neutral or mixed feelings
Does not agree at all	(4) Positive feelings

Stigma (S)

Derived from responses to two items *You feel your pride would be affected* (if you claimed benefits). *You would feel you were accepting charity.*

(1) Strong stigma (agrees or agrees strongly with both)

(2) Some stigma

(3) No stigma (disagrees with both or cannot say)

Social approval (SA)

Derived from statements about approval or disapproval from friends, relatives and other people they know.

(1) Approval which matters

(2) Disapproval which matters

(3) Mixture of approval and disapproval

(4) No approval which matters

Encouragement to claim (E)

(1) Personally advised or encouraged

(2) Not advised but received SCPR letter

(3) No advice or letter before claim

Sex and partnership (SP)

(1) Lives in partnership—claimant most probably male

(2) No partnership—claimant is male

(3) No partnership—claimant is female

Children (C)

(1) Has dependent children

(2) Has no dependent children

Age of claimant

(1) Under 25

(2) 25–49

(3) 50 up to retirement age

(4) Retirement age to 69

(5) 70 or over

Employment status of claimant (ES)

(1) Employed

(2) Unemployed

(3) Other not working

Table 1

Claiming behaviour cross-classified by

  Age

  Stigma (S)

  Beliefs and Feelings (BF)

Age has 3 categories—<50, 50-retired, retired.

Stigma has 2 categories—some stigma, no stigma attached to claiming process.

Beliefs and Feelings has 4 categories—agrees strongly, agrees, does not agree, can't say—to the statement.

Model	Deviance	Degrees of Freedom	Conclusion
Null	59.26	23	Does not fit
Age	44.22	21	Does not fit
S	58.38	22	Does not fit
BF	55.84	20	Does not fit
Age + S	44.13	20	Does not fit
Age + BF	38.70	18	Does not fit
S + BF	53.75	19	Does not fit
Age + S + Age.S	43.74	18	Does not fit
Age + BF + Age.BF	21.65	12	Does not fit
S + BF + S.BF	46.30	16	Does not fit
Age + S + BF	38.25	17	Does not fit
Age + S + BF + Age.S	37.63	15	Does not fit
Age + S + BF + Age.BF	21.20	11	Does not fit
Age + S + BF + S.BF	28.67	14	Does not fit
Age + S + BF + Age.S + Age.BF	20.89	9	Does not fit
Age + S + BF + Age.S + S.BF	26.66	12	Does not fit
Age + S + BF + Age.BF + S.BF	12.02	8	Fits at 10%
Age + S + BF + Age.S + Age.BF + S.BF	10.82	6	Fits at 5%
Age + S + BF + Age.S + Age.BF + S.BF + Age.S.BF	0	0	

The last model listed is the *saturated model* which will, by definition, fit exactly (since all possible parameters are included in the model). Note that the models are *hierarchical* in the sense that if a 2-way interaction is included in the model, then both main effects must also appear. The interpretation of a 2-way interaction is that the effect of one of the factors on claiming behaviour is not constant at all levels of the other factor. (For example, the presence of an Age.BF interaction indicates that the effect of age on propensity to claim is not the same for people who agree strongly as for those who disagree with the BF statement). In this case, then, the preferred mode is

Age + S + BF + Age.BF + S.BF.

The parameter estimates are as follows:

Parameter	Estimate	Standard error of estimate
Grand mean	1.070	0.462
Age—level 2 (Age(2))	−3.105	0.873
Age(3)	−2.163	0.670
Stig(2)	0.297	0.646
BF(2)	−0.186	1.023
BF(3)	−14.050	74.930
BF(4)	0.153	1.594
Age(2).BF(2)	1.751	1.313
Age(2).BF(3)	−6.980	82.840
Age(2).BF(4)	2.619	1.545
Age(3).BF(2)	1.902	1.318
Age(3).BF(3)	4.620	1.458
Age(3).BF(4)	1.143	1.736
Stig(2).BF(2)	−0.827	1.102
Stig(2).BF(3)	11.830	74.930
Stig(2).BF(4)	−1.740	1.590

Table 2

Claiming behaviour cross-classified by

    Perceived Need (PN)   2 levels

    Social Approval (SA)   3 levels

    Employment Status (ES)   3 levels

Preferred model: PN + SA (Deviance 5.152 Degrees of freedom 14)

Parameter	Estimate	Standard error of estimate
Grand mean	−1.354	0.391
PN(2)	1.625	0.422
SA(2)	10.970	32.680
SA(3)	−0.128	0.388

Table 3

Claiming behaviour cross-classified by

    Perceived Eligibility (PE)   2 levels

    Social Approval (SA)   3 levels

    Sex and partnership (SP)   3 levels

Preferred model: PE + SA (Scaled Deviance 11.47 Degrees of freedom 14)

Parameter	Estimate	Standard error of estimate
Grand mean	0.1070	0.304
PE(2)	10.570	31.960
SA(2)	−0.094	0.371
SA(3)	−0.875	0.370

Table 4

Claiming behaviour cross-classified by

    Encouragement to claim (E)   3 levels

    Perceived Need (PN)   2 levels

    Age (AGE)   3 levels

Preferred model: PN + E (Scaled Deviance 18.62 Degrees of freedom 14)

Parameter	Estimate	Standard error of estimate
Grand mean	−0.497	0.590
PN(2)	1.416	0.412
E(2)	−0.453	0.535
E(3)	−2.601	0.898

Table 5

Claiming behaviour cross-classified by

    Encouragement to Claim (E)   3 levels

    Perceived Eligibility (PE)   2 levels

    Age (AGE)   3 levels

Preferred model: E + AGE + E.AGE (Deviance 13.17
Degrees of freedom 9)

Parameter	Estimate	Standard error of estimate
Grand mean	1.705	0.769
E(2)	−1.500	0.821
E(3)	−2.398	1.158
AGE(2)	−1.705	1.261
AGE(3)	−2.110	1.193
E(2).AGE(2)	0.776	1.390
E(2).AGE(3)	1.992	1.297
E(3).AGE(2)	−9.054	62.02
E(3).AGE(3)	−8.230	67.50

Table 6

Claiming behaviour cross-classified by

    Encouragement to Claim (E)   3 levels

    Perceived Need (PN)   2 levels

    Perceived Eligibility (PE)   2 levels

Preferred model: E + PN + PE + E.PN (Deviance 7.861
Degrees of freedom 5)

Parameter	Estimate	Standard error of estimate
Grand mean	1.687	0.614
E(2)	−0.834	0.646
E(3)	−2.662	0.993
PN(2)	−11.940	76.780
PE(2)	−0.961	0.402
E(2).PN(2)	10.790	76.780
E(3).PN(2)	1.802	97.240

Table 7

Claiming behaviour cross-classified by

    Encouragement to claim (E)   3 levels

    Social Approval (SA)   3 levels

    Age (AGE)   3 levels

Preferred model: E + AGE + E.AGE (Deviance 10.86 Degrees of freedom 9)

Parameter	Estimate	Standard error of estimate
Grand mean	1.705	0.769
E(2)	−1.500	0.821
E(3)	−2.398	1.158
AGE(2)	−2.398	1.446
AGE(3)	−2.110	1.193
E(2).AGE(2)	0.969	1.560
E(2).AGE(3)	1.992	1.297
E(3).AGE(2)	−8.336	61.270
E(3).AGE(3)	−8.230	67.500

The 7 separate analyses may then be synthesised to give the conclusions described in the main text.

References

Baker, R J, Nelder, J A. The GLIM System, Release 3, Generalised Linear Inter-active Modelling. Numerical Algorithms Group, Oxford, 1978.

Kendall, M, Stuart A. Vol. 2 Inference and Relationship, The Advanced Theory of Statistics, Charles Griffin and Co Ltd, 1967.

APPENDIX III
STUDY DOCUMENTS

- Letter advising non-claimants about probable eligibility
- Consent form for record check
- Questionnaire

Dear

In the autumn of last year you were kind enough to take part in a study we carried out for the London Borough of Hackney. The main aim of the study was to establish the extent to which people in the borough are receiving their full entitlement of state or local authority benefits, rebates or allowances.

As we explained at the time, the study is being carried out primarily for research purposes. However, you said that you would like to know if we thought you might be eligible for any of the benefits we were investigating. Having looked at the information you gave us, we think that you might be eligible for [SB, HB, FIS].

We should stress, though, that these are not official assessments and we cannot guarantee that this would be the outcome if you were to make a formal application. Should you wish to enquire further we have enclosed a list of addresses where you can obtain further information.

We apologise for the delay in writing to you but as you can probably appreciate, it has taken us some time to do the assessments for all the people we interviewed. We must also emphasise that our assessments are based on the information you gave us last autumn. Obviously any change in your circumstances since then will have an impact on whether or not you may be eligible. There have also been some changes in the way benefits are assessed since last November and again these may have affected your possible entitlement. However, we do think it is worth you making enquiries should you wish to do so.

Thank you very much for taking part in the study, we were very grateful indeed for your help.

Yours sincerely

Judith England
Project Researcher

Head Office: 35 Northampton Square London EC1V 0AX. Tel: 01-250 1866
Northern Field Office: Charazel House Gainford Darlington Co. Durham DL2 3EG. Tel: 0325 730 888

SOCIAL AND COMMUNITY PLANNING RESEARCH

P.808

HACKNEY BENEFIT STUDY

Authorisation Form

I am willing for the DHSS/Hackney Housing Benefit Office to give SCPR information about the outcome of any claim I might make for

....

Signed ....
Name ....
Address ....
....
....
....

scpr
SOCIAL AND COMMUNITY PLANNING RESEARCH

Head Office: 35 Northampton Square London EC1V 0AX. Tel: 01-250 1866
Northern Field Office: Charazel House Gainford Darlington Co. Durham DL2 3EG. Tel: 0325 730 888

P.808   HACKNEY BENEFIT STUDY   July 1984
                    Follow-up survey

(201-04) ☐☐☐☐   (205) ☐   (206) ☐   (207-08) |0|2| (209) |1|
Address Serial No.   H/Hold   Claim   Card No.   Sample
                     No.   Unit No   Group

Time interview started ....

		Col./Code	Skip to
1.	I'd like to ask first of all about any changes there have been in your household since we last talked to you - that is, since _____ (INT MONTH)		
a)	Can I just check, were you living at this address in _____ (INT MONTH), or have you moved since then?	(210)	
	Still at same address	1	Q.2
	Moved from 1st interview address	A	
	IF MOVED (CODE 2) AT a)		
b)	Have you moved just once, or have you moved more than once since then?		
	One move only	2 ⎱	c)
	More than 1 move	3 ⎰	
c)	Why did you move from your previous address? (IF MORE THAN ONE MOVE: the address where you lived when we saw you last time?).		

			Col./ Code	Skip to
	IF HOUSEHOLDER (i.e. CLAIM UNIT NO = 1) NON-HOUSEHOLDERS SKIP TO Q.3			
2.a)	(Can I just check again) who else lives here regularly with you as members of your household? No one, lives alone		(211) 0	
	ENTER RELATIONSHIP, AGE, SEX, MARITAL STATUS AND ACTIVITY STATUS OF EACH HOUSEHOLD MEMBER.			

PERSON NUMBER	Relationship to Respondent	Sex M F	Age last birthday	Marital Status M LM S W DS	Activity Status Emp F/T P/T	Un emp	At Sch	FT Ed	Not Wkng	
1	Respondent	1 2		1 2 3 4 5	1 2	3	4	5	6	(212-18)
2		1 2		1 2 3 4 5	1 2	3	4	5	6	(219-25)
3		1 2		1 2 3 4 5	1 2	3	4	5	6	(226-32)
4		1 2		1 2 3 4 5	1 2	3	4	5	6	(233-39)
5		1 2		1 2 3 4 5	1 2	3	4	5	6	(240-46)
6		1 2		1 2 3 4 5	1 2	3	4	5	6	(247-53)
7		1 2		1 2 3 4 5	1 2	3	4	5	6	(254-60)
8		1 2		1 2 3 4 5	1 2	3	4	5	6	(261-67)
9		1 2		1 2 3 4 5	1 2	3	4	5	6	(268-74)

b)	Was there anyone living with you in _____(INT. MONTH) who is no longer living with you?		(275)	
		No	1	See c)
		Yes, ENTER Relationship(s)	2	
	....		(276)	
			(277)	
	IF LIVES WITH OTHERS IF LIVES ALONE, SKIP TO Q.4			
c)	And have any of the people in your household come to live with you since _____(INT. MONTH)?			
		No	1	Q.4
		Yes, ENTER PERSON NO(S)	2	Q.4
	(278) (279) (280)			
			301-06	Rpt
			307-08	Card 03

			Col./Code	Skip to
	IF NON-HOUSEHOLDER (i.e. CLAIM UNIT NO. = 2 - 8)			
3.a)	ENTER SEX		(309)	
		Male	1	
		Female	2	
b)	Can you tell me, what was your age last birthday?		(310-11)	
		ENTER AGE		
c)	Are you.... READ OUT ...		(312)	
		Married	1	d)
		Living as married	2	e)
		Single	3	
		Widowed	4	f)
		Divorced/Separated	5	
	IF MARRIED (CODE 1 AT c)		(313)	
d)	Does your husband/wife live here with you?	Yes	1	e)
		No	2	f)
	IF LIVES WITH SPOUSE/PARTNER			
e)	How old was your husband/wife partner last birthday?		(314-15)	
		ENTER AGE		
	ASK ALL		(316)	
f)	(Can I just check) do you have any children who live here with you?	Yes	1	g)
		No	2	h)
	IF HAS CHILDREN (CODE 1 at f)			
g)	Are any of your children ...READ OUT		(317)	
	ENTER '0' IF NONE	of pre-school age ENTER NUMBER		
			(318)	
		at school ENTER NUMBER		
			(319)	
		aged 16 to 19 and in full ENTER NUMBER time education (other than school)		
	ASK ALL		(320)	
h)	At present are you ....READ OUT ...	in full time employment (30 hrs+)	1	
		in part time employment	2	
		unemployed	3	
		in full time education	4	
		or not working	5	
	IF LIVES WITH SPOUSE/PARTNER OTHERS SKIP TO Q.4		(321)	
i)	And at present is your husband/wife/ partner ....READ OUT ...	in full time employment (30 hrs+)	1	
		in part time employment	2	
		unemployed	3	Q.4
		in full time education	4	
		or not working	5	

- 4 -

		Col./Code	Skip to
ASK ALL			
4.a)	As I have explained, we would like to talk to you more about some of the benefits you might be able to claim. So could I first check, have you (or your wife/husband/partner) made a claim for _____ (MAIN BENEFIT) since _____ (INT. MNTH)	(322)	
	Yes	1	b)
	No	2	g)
IF YES AT a)			
b)	Can I just check have you claimed _____ (MAIN BENEFIT) once or more than once since _____ (INT. MNTH)?	(323)	
	Once only	1	c)
	More than once	2	
c)	When did you (first) apply? Was it .....READ OUT	(324)	
	before Christmas	1	d)
	or after Christmas	2	
	(Can't remember)	3	e)
d)	Can you remember approximately which month it was? Enter month_____	(325-26)	See e)
	Can't remember	08	e)
IF MAY OR LATER **IF BEFORE MAY SKIP TO Q.5**			
e)	We recently sent you a letter about benefits for which we thought you might be eligible. Did this have any influence on your decision to apply?	(327)	
	Yes	1	f)
	No	2	
	Can't say	3	Q.5
	Don't remember receiving it	4	
IF YES AT d)			
f)	What was it, in particular, that influenced you? PROBE FULLY AND RECORD VERBATIM.		
IF NO AT a)		(328)	
g)	Can I just check, are you receiving _____ (MAIN BENEFIT) at present? Yes	1	h)
	No	2	Q.38
IF YES AT g)		(329)	
h)	So were you receiving main benefit when we interviewed you last time? Yes	1	i)
	No	2	RECHECK Q.4a)
IF YES AT h)			
i)	For how long have you been receiving _____ (MAIN BENEFIT) ENTER LENGTH OF TIME _____ yrs _____ mnths	(330)	
INTERVIEWER CHECK (IF YES AT 4h)		(331)	
	SECOND benefit listed	1	Q.82
	No OTHER benefit listed		END INTERVIEW

100

			Col./Code	Skip to

ALL CLAIMANTS

IF MORE THAN ONE CLAIM SINCE INTERVIEW DATE,
Q.5 REFERS TO FIRST CLAIM

5.a) What was the result of your (first) claim?
Were you ...READ OUT ...

(332)

Given the benefit	1	Q.6
or was your claim turned down	2	b)
(not yet heard)	3	Q.6

IF CLAIM TURNED DOWN

b) Were you given any reasons why your claim was turned down?

(333)

Yes	1	c)
No	2	f)
Can't remember	3	

IF YES AT b)

c) What were the reasons they gave?
PROBE FULLY AND RECORD VERBATIM.

(334)

d) Were you satisfied with this explanation or not?

Yes, satisfied	1	f)
No, not satisfied	2	e)

IF NOT SATISFIED AT d)

e) Why were you not satisfied?
PROBE FULLY AND RECORD VERBATIM.

ALL WHOSE CLAIM WAS TURNED DOWN

f) How did you feel when your claim was turned down?
PROBE FULLY AND RECORD VERBATIM.

		Col./ Code	Skip to

ALL CLAIMANTS

6.a) Thinking back, what was it that made you (your husband/wife/partner) decide to apply for _____ (MAIN BENEFIT) (the first time)?
PROBE FULLY AND RECORD VERBATIM.

b) Did anything particular happen that finally influenced your decision to claim?

	Col./Code	Skip to
	(335)	
Yes	1	
No	2	SEE Q.7
Can't remember	3	Q.7

IF YES AT b)

c) What was it that happened?

SEE Q.7

		Col./ Code	Skip to

IF MORE THAN ONE CLAIM FOR MAIN BENEFIT SINCE INTERVIEW DATE
(CODE 2 AT Q.4b)   OTHERS SKIP TO Q.10

7.a) Thinking about the second time you applied
for _____ (MAIN BENEFIT),
when did you make the claim. Was it ...READ OUT...

		(336)	
before Christmas		1 ⎫	b)
or after Christmas		2 ⎭	
(Can't remember)		3	c)

b) Can you remember approximately which
month it was?

		(337-38)	
Enter month _____			See c)
Can't remember		08	c)

IF MAY OR LATER   IF BEFORE MAY SKIP TO Q.8

c) We recently sent you a letter about
benefits for which we thought you
might be eligible. Did this have
any influence on your decision to apply?

		(339)	
Yes		1	d)
No		2 ⎫	
Can't say		3 ⎬	Q.8
Don't remember receiving it		4 ⎭	

IF YES AT d)

d) What was it, in particular, that influenced you?
PROBE FULLY AND RECORD VERBATIM.

				Col./ Code	Skip to
8.a)	What was the result of your claim? Were you...READ OUT...			(340)	
			Given the benefit	1	Q.9
		or was your claim turned down		2	b)
			(not yet heard)	3	Q.9
	IF CLAIM TURNED DOWN			(341)	
	b) Were you given any reasons why your claim was turned down?		Yes	1	c)
			No	2	f)
			Can't remember	3	
	IF YES AT b)				
	c) What were the reasons they have? PROBE FULLY AND RECORD VERBATIM.				
	d) Were you satisfied with this explanation or not?			(342)	
			Yes, satisfied	1	f)
			No, not satisfied	2	e)
	IF NOT SATISFIED AT d)				
	e) Why were you not satisfied? PROBE FULLY AND RECORD VERBATIM.				
	ALL WHOSE CLAIM WAS TURNED DOWN				
	f) How did you feel when your claim was turned down? PROBE FULLY AND RECORD VERBATIM.				

	ALL CLAIMANTS	Col./ Code	Skip to
9.a)	Thinking back, what was it that made you (your husband/wife/partner) decide to apply for (____MAIN BENEFIT) the second time? PROBE FULLY AND RECORD VERBATIM.		

b)	Did anything particular happen that finally influenced your decision to claim?
	                                        Yes
	                                        No
	                        Can't remember
		(343)
		1
		2
		3
			Q.10

	IF YES AT b) c) What was it that happened?		

- 10 -

ALL CLAIMANTS

10.a) Before you applied for _____ (MAIN BENEFIT) (the first time) did you (or your husband/wife/partner) see or hear anything about the benefit. Did you... READ OUT...

	YES	NO	Col./Code	Skip to
See or hear something on the radio or TV	1	2	(344)	
read something in a newspaper or magazine	1	2	(345)	
read a booklet or leaflet about the benefit	1	2	(346)	
read some GLC information about the benefit put through your door	1	2	(347)	
see a notice or poster about the benefit	1	2	(348)	
or see or hear anything else (SPECIFY) _____	1	2	(349)	

IF YES TO ANY AT a)   IF NO TO ALL AT a) SKIP TO d)

b) Did (any of) the things you saw or heard influence your decision to make a claim?

		(350)	
Yes	1		c)
No	2		d)

IF YES AT b)

c) What influenced your decision?
RECORD SPECIFIC DETAILS OF INFORMATION SOURCE

d) Can I just check, did the previous interview have any effect on your (or your husband/wife/partners') decision to apply?

		(351)	
Yes	1		e)
No	2		Q.11

IF YES AT d)

e) In what way did it influence you?

		Col./ Code	Skip to
	ALL CLAIMANTS		
11.a)	Before you applied for _____(MAIN BENEFIT) (the first time), did you (or your husband/wife/partner) talk to any of your relatives about making a claim? I mean apart from relatives that live with you. Yes No	(352) 1 2	Q.12
	IF YES AT a)		
b)	Which relatives did you talk to about it?		

ENTER RELATIONSHIP TO RESPONDENT	(353)	(357)	(361)	(365)
FOR EACH ASK				
c) How did _____(REL) feel about you claiming _____ (MAIN BENEFIT)? Do you think he/she generally approved or disapproved?	(354)	(358)	(362)	(366)
Approved	1	1	1	1
Disapproved	2	2	2	2
No feelings expressed	3	3	3	3
d) How much did _____ (RELATIVE)'s views about this matter to you? Did they matter ... READ OUT ...	(355)	(359)	(363)	(367)
a great deal	1	1	1	1
quite a lot	2	2	2	2
a little	3	3	3	3
not very much	4	4	4	4
or not at all	5	5	5	5
e) Does _____(RELATIVE) know that you made a claim for _____ (MAIN BENEFIT)?	(356)	(360)	(364)	(368)
Yes	1	1	1	1
No	2	2	2	2

(369-80) Blank
(401-06) Repeat
(407-08) CARD 04

- 12 -

						Col./ Code	Skip to
12.a)	ALL CLAIMANTS Do you have any (other) relatives you are close to? DO NOT INCLUDE HOUSEHOLD MEMBERS. Yes No					(409) 1 2	Q.13
	IF YES AT a) b) Which other relatives are you close to?						
	ENTER RELATIONSHIP TO RESPONDENT						
	FOR EACH ASK	(410)	(415)	(420)	(425)		
	c) Does _____ (RELATIVE) know you have claimed _____ (MAIN BENEFIT)? Yes No	(411) 1 d) 2 e)	(416) 1 d) 2 e)	(421) 1 d) 2 e)	(426) 1 d) 2 e)		
	IF YES AT c) d) How does _____ (RELATIVE) feel about your claiming _____ (MAIN BENEFIT). Do you think he/she generally approves or disapproves? Approves Disapproves No feelings expressed	(412) 1 2 } f) 3	(417) 1 2 } f) 3	(422) 1 2 } f) 3	(427) 1 2 } f) 3		
	IF NO AT c) e) How would _____ (REL) feel about you claiming _____ (MAIN BENEFIT). Do you think he/she would generally approve or disapprove? Approve Disapprove Don't know	(413) 1 2 } f) 3	(418) 1 2 } f) 3	(423) 1 2 } f) 3	(428) 1 2 } f) 3		
	ALL f) How much do _____ (REL)'s views matter to you. Do they matter ..READ OUT.. a great deal quite a lot a little not very much or not at all	(414) 1 2 3 4 5	(419) 1 2 3 4 5	(424) 1 2 3 4 5	(429) 1 2 3 4 5		

- 13 -

		Col./Code	Skip to

ALL CLAIMANTS

13.a) Before you applied for _____ (MAIN BENEFIT), did you (or your husband/wife/partner) talk to any friends or neighbours you are close to about making a claim?

(430)

Yes — 1
No — 2 — Q.14

IF YES AT (a)

b) Which friends did you talk to about it?

ENTER IDENTIFIER FOR EACH ASK	1 (431)	2 (435)	3 (439)	4 (443)
c) How did ____(FRIEND) feel about you claiming ____(MAIN BENEFIT)? Do you think he/she generally approved or disapproved?	(432)	(436)	(440)	(444)
Approved	1	1	1	1
Disapproved	2	2	2	2
No feelings expressed	3	3	3	3
d) How much did ____(FRIEND)'s views matter to you? Did they matter ...READ OUT...	(433)	(437)	(441)	(445)
a great deal	1	1	1	1
quite a lot	2	2	2	2
a little	3	3	3	3
not very much	4	4	4	4
or not at all	5	5	5	5
e) Does ____(FRIEND) know that you made a claim for ____(MAIN BENEFIT)?	(434)	(438)	(442)	(446)
Yes	1	1	1	1
No	2	2	2	2

- 14 -

						Col./Code	Skip to
14.a)	Do you have any (other) friends or neighbours you are close to?					(447)	
					Yes	1	
					No	2	Q.15

IF YES AT a)

b) Which friends or neighbours are you close to?

ENTER IDENTIFIER	1 (448)	2 (453)	3 (458)	4 (463)
FOR EACH ASK c) Does ____ (FRIEND) know you have claimed ____ (MAIN BENEFIT)? Yes No	(449) 1 d) 2 e)	(454) 1 d) 2 e)	(459) 1 d) 2 e)	(464) 1 d) 2 e)
IF YES AT c) d) How does ____ (FRIEND) feel about your claiming ____ (MAIN BENEFIT). Do you think he/she generally approves or disapproves? Approves Disapproves No feelings expressed	(450) 1 2 } f) 3	(455) 1 2 } f) 3	(460) 1 2 } f) 3	(465) 1 2 } f) 3
IF NO AT c) e) How would ____ (FRIEND) feel about your claiming ____ (MAIN BENEFIT). Do you think he/she would generally approve or disapprove? Approve Disapprove Don't know	(451) 1 2 } f) 3	(456) 1 2 } f) 3	(461) 1 2 } f) 3	(466) 1 2 } f) 3
ALL f) How much does ____ (FR)'s views matter to you? Do they matter ... READ OUT ... a great deal quite a lot a little not very much or not at all	(452) 1 2 3 4 5	(457) 1 2 3 4 5	(462) 1 2 3 4 5	(467) 1 2 3 4 5

			Col./Code	Skip to
	ALL CLAIMANTS WHO HAVE MENTIONED CLOSE FRIENDS OR RELATIVES OTHERS SKIP TO Q.16		(468)	
15.a)	Are there any relatives or friends you've mentioned who you would <u>not</u> want to know you claimed ____ (MAIN BENEFIT)?	Yes No	1 2	b) Q.16
	IF YES AT a)		(469)	
b)	Which relatives or friends are these? ENTER RELATIONSHIP OR IDENTIFIER.		(470)	
			(471)	
			(472-80) (501-06) (507-08)	Blank Repeat Card 05
16.a)	Before you decided to apply, did you (or your husband/wife/partner) talk to any of the following people about making a claim for ____ (MAIN BENEFIT)? READ OUT IN TURN			
	A housing officer, social worker or any other official,	1 2	(509)	
	Someone at the Citizens Advice Bureau or Centreprise,	1 2	(510)	
	Someone on the GLC benefit bus,	1 2	(511)	
	Or anyone else you've not mentioned so far (SPECIFY)	1 2	(512)	
	IF YES TO ANY AT a) IF NO TO ALL AT a) SKIP TO INTERVIEWER CHECK BELOW		(513)	
b)	Did (any of) the people you talked to influence your decision to make a claim?	Yes No	1 2	c) d)
	IF YES AT b)			
c)	Who influenced your decision to claim? ENTER ROLE/ORGANISATION			
d)	Did (any of) the people you talked to encourage you to make a claim?	Yes No	(514) 1 2	e) See INTER-VIEWER CHECK BELOW
	IF YES AT d)			
e)	Who encouraged you to make a claim? ENTER RELATIONSHIP OR ROLE/ORGANISATION			
	INTERVIEWER CHECK		(515)	
	MAIN BENEFIT IS SUPPLEMENTARY BENEFIT		1	Q.17
	MAIN BENEFIT IS HOUSING BENEFIT		2	Q.25
	MAIN BENEFIT IS FAMILY INCOME SUPPLEMENT		3	Q.30

			Col./ Code	Skip to

MAIN BENEFIT: SUPPLEMENTARY BENEFIT

17. I'd like to spend a few minutes talking about your application for supplementary benefit. For each part of the procedure I mention I would like you to tell me how you felt about it.

a) When you claimed you had to apply to the Social Security Office to verify that you were eligible. Did you have any strong feelings one way or the other about applying to the Social Security Office.

(516)

Yes A   b)
No   4   See Q18

IF YES AT a)

b) How did you feel about it?

INTERVIEWER RATING   +3   +2   +1   0   -1   -2   -3

PENSIONERS ONLY (RESPONDENT OR SPOUSE 65/60 OR OVER)
NON-PENSIONERS SKIP TO Q.19

18.a) When you claimed you would have had an interview with a Social Security official. Did you have any strong feelings one way or the other about that?

(517)

Yes A   b)
No   4   c)

IF YES AT a)

b) How did you feel about it?

INTERVIEWER RATING   +3   +2   +1   0   -1   -2   -3

c) Where did you have the interview?
Was it... READ OUT ...

(518)

At home   1 } d)
or at the social security office   2 }

d) Did you have any strong feelings either way about having the interview at home/at the social security office?

(519)

Yes A   e)
No   4   Q.22A

IF YES AT d)

e) How did you feel about having the interview at home/at the social security office?

INTERVIEWER RATING   +3   +2   +1   0   -1   -2   -3   Q.22A

			Col./ Code	Skip to
	NON-PENSIONERS			
19.a)	Can I just check, when you (your husband/wife/partner) claimed supplementary benefit, were you registered as unemployed or not?	Yes No	(520) 1 2	b) Q.20
	IF YES AT a)			
b)	You would have had to go to the Unemployment Benefit Office for a claim form. Did you have any strong feelings one way or the other about that?	Yes No	(521) A 4	c) Q.20
	IF YES AT b)			
c)	How did you feel about it?			
	INTERVIEWER RATING +3 +2 +1 0 -1 -2 -3			
	ALL NON-PENSIONERS			
20.a)	When you (your husband/wife/partner) applied you had to fill in the claim form. Did you have any strong feelings one way or the other about that?	Yes No	(522) A 4	b) Q.21
	IF YES AT a)			
b)	How did you feel about it?			
	INTERVIEWER RATING +3 +2 +1 0 -1 -2 -3			
21.a)	Did you have an interview with someone from the social security office when you made a claim?	Yes No	(523) 1 2	b) Q.22B
	IF YES AT a)			
b)	Did you have any strong feelings one way or the other about having an interview?	Yes No	(524) A 4	c) Q.22A
	IF YES AT b)			
c)	How did you feel about it?			
	INTERVIEWER RATING +3 +2 +1 0 -1 -2 -3			

- 18 -

		Col./ Code	Skip to
22.A)	**IF HAD INTERVIEW (PENSIONER OR CODE 1 AT Q.21a)** In your interview, the social security official asked you quite a few questions. I'd like to know how you felt about having to answer some of those questions.		
22.B)	**IF DID NOT HAVE INTERVIEW (CODE 2 AT Q.21a)** When you completed the claim form you had to answer quite a few questions. I'd like to know how you felt about having to answer some of those questions.		
	Did you feel strongly one way or the other about the questions on ...	(525)	
a)	Your weekly income, its amount and where it comes from? Yes No	A 4	b) c)
	IF YES AT a) b) How did you feel about those questions?		
	+3 +2 +1 0 -1 -2 -3		
c)	Your savings, their amount and where you have them saved? Yes No	(526) A 4	d) e)
	IF YES AT c) d) How did you feel about those questions?		
	+3 +2 +1 0 -1 -2 -3		
e)	Your health and the health of those living with you? Yes No	(527) A 4	f) g)
	IF YES AT e) f) How did you feel about those questions?		
	+3 +2 +1 0 -1 -2 -3		
g)	How much rent or mortgage you pay and who you pay it to? Yes No	(528) A 4	h) i)
	IF YES AT g) h) How did you feel about those questions?		
	+3 +2 +1 0 -1 -2 -3		
i)	Your family, whether you get any income from them and how much the income amounts to? Yes No	(529) A 4	j) Q.23
	IF YES AT i) j) How did you feel about those questions?		
	+3 +2 +1 0 -1 -2 -3		

114

- 19 -

		Col./Code	Skip to

ALL SUPPLEMENTARY BENEFIT CLAIMANTS

23. When you claimed you would have had to give some <u>evidence</u> of your financial circumstances such as your savings, your rent book, your order book etc. Did you have any strong feelings one way or the other about this?

    Yes   (530) A   b)
    No   4   Q.24

IF YES AT a)
b) How did you feel about it.

INTERVIEWER RATING   +3   +2   +1   0   -1   -2   -3

24. a) How did you feel about the way you were treated by the officials from the social security office?

    No contact with them   (531) A   b)
        4

INTERVIEWER RATING   +3   +2   +1   0   -1   -2   -3

b) Can I just check did you go to the social security office when you made your claim?

    Yes   (532) A   c)
    No   4   See Q.35

IF YES AT b)
c) How did you feel about that?

INTERVIEWER RATING   +3   +2   +1   0   -1   -2   -3

d) Were there other people there waiting to be seen?

    Yes   (533) A   e)
    No   4   See Q.35

IF YES AT d)
e) How did you feel about being in their company.

INTERVIEWER RATING   +3   +2   +1   0   -1   -2   -3   → See Q.35

- 20 -

			Col./Code	Skip to
	MAIN BENEFIT : HOUSING BENEFIT			
25.	I'd like to spend a few minutes talking about your application for your rent or rate rebate. For each part of the procedure I mention I would like you to tell me how you felt about it.			
	When you claimed you had to apply to the Council's rebate office to verify that you were eligible. Did you have any strong feelings one way or the other about applying to the rebate office.		(534)	
		Yes	A	b)
		No	4	c)
	IF YES AT a) b) How did you feel about it.			
	INTERVIEWER RATING +3 +2 +1 0 -1 -2 -3			
c)	You would also have had to fill in a claim form. Did you have any strong feelings one way or the other about filling in the claim form?		(535)	
		Yes	A	d)
		No	4	Q.26
	IF YES AT c) d) How did you feel about it.			
	INTERVIEWER RATING +4 +2 +1 0 -1 -2 -3			

- 21 -

			Col./ Code	Skip to
26.	When you completed the claim form you had to answer quite a few questions. I'd like to know how you felt about having to answer those questions. Did you feel strongly one way or the other about the questions on ... READ OUT ...			
a)	Your weekly income, it's amounts and where it comes from?	Yes	(536) A	b)
		No	4	c)
	IF YES AT a) b) How did you feel about those questions?			
	INTERVIEWER RATING +3 +2 +1 0 -1 -2 -3			
c)	Your savings and the amount of interest you receive	Yes	(537) A	d)
		No	4	e)
	IF YES AT c) d) How did you feel about those questions?			
	INTERVIEWER RATING +3 +2 +1 0 -1 -2 -3			
e)	Details of your family and other people living with you	Yes	(538) A	f)
		No	4	g)
	IF YES AT e) f) How did you feel about those questions?			
	INTERVIEWER RATING +3 +2 +1 0 -1 -2 -3			
g)	Your rates, rent and what it covers?	Yes	(539) A	h)
		No	4	Q.27
	IF YES AT g) h) How did you feel about those questions?			
	INTERVIEWER RATING +3 +2 +1 0 -1 -2 -3			

			Col./ Code	Skip to
	ALL HOUSING BENEFIT CLAIMANTS		(540)	
27.a)	When you claimed you would have had to give some <u>evidence</u> of your financial circumstances such as your rent or rates, your income, etc. Did you have any strong feelings one way or the other about this?	Yes	A	b)
		No	4	See c)
	IF YES AT a) b) How did you feel about it?			
	INTERVIEWER RATING +3 +2 +1 0 -1 -2 -3			
			(541)	
	IF RESPONDENT OR SPOUSE EMPLOYED OTHERS SKIP TO Q.28			
c)	You would also have had to give the name of your (and your husband/wife/partner's) employer. Did you have any strong feelings one way or the other about that?	Yes	A	d)
		No	4	Q.28
	IF YES AT c) d) How did you feel about it?			
	INTERVIEWER RATING +3 +2 +1 0 -1 -2 -3			
			(542)	
28.a)	When you applied for your rent or rate rebate, did you have any contact with officials from the Council's rebate office?	Yes	A	b)
		No	4	Q.29
	IF YES AT a) b) How did you feel about the way you were treated by the officials?			
	INTERVIEWER RATING +3 +2 +1 0 -1 -2 -3			
			(543)	
29.a)	Did you go to the rebate office for any reason?	Yes	A	b)
	IF YES AT a) b) How did you feel about that?	No	4	See Q35
	INTERVIEWER RATING +3 +2 +1 0 -1 -2 -3			
			(544)	
	c) Were there other people there waiting to be seen?	Yes	A	d)
		No	4	See Q35
	IF YES AT c) d) How did you feel about being in their company?			
	INTERVIEWER RATING +3 +2 +1 0 -1 -2 -3 ⟶			See Q35

MAIN BENEFIT : FAMILY INCOME SUPPLEMENT

30. I'd like to spend a few minutes talking about your application for Family Income Supplement. For each part of the procedure I mention I would like you to tell me how you feel about it.

a) When you claimed you had to apply to the DHSS to verify that you were eligible. Did you have any strong feelings one way or the other about applying to the DHSS?

	Col./Code	Skip to
Yes	(545) A	b)
No	4	c)

IF YES AT a)
b) How did you feel about it?

INTERVIEWER RATING   +3   +2   +1   0   -1   -2   -3

c) You would also have had to fill in a claim form. Did you have any strong feelings one way or the other about filling in the claim form?

	Col./Code	Skip to
Yes	(546) A	d)
No	4	e)

IF YES AT c)
d) How did you feel about it?

INTERVIEWER RATING   +3   +2   +1   0   -1   -2   -3

e) Your claim would have been dealt with by a DHSS office in Blackpool? Did you have any strong feelings one way or the other about this?

	Col./Code	Skip to
Yes	(547) A	f)
No	4	Q.31

IF YES AT a)
f) How did you feel about it?

INTERVIEWER RATING   +3   +2   +1   0   -1   -2   -3

- 24 -

			Col./ Code	Skip to

31. When you completed the claim form you had to answer quite a few questions. I'd like to know how you felt about having to answer those questions. Did you feel strongly one way or the other about the questions on ... READ OUT ...

a) Your earnings from employment?   Yes (548) A   b)
                                       No   4   c)

IF YES AT a)
b) How did you feel about those questions?

INTERVIEWER RATING   +3   +2   +1   0   -1   -2   -3

c) Your savings and the amount of interest you receive?   Yes (549) A   d)
                                                          No   4   e)

IF YES AT c)
d) How did you feel about those questions?

INTERVIEWER RATING   +3   +2   +1   0   -1   -2   -3

e) Your other sources of income such as benefits, maintenance, income from lodgers, etc.   Yes (550) A   f)
                                                                                           No   4   g)

IF YES AT e)
f) How did you feel about those questions?

INTERVIEWER RATING   +3   +2   +1   0   -1   -2   -3

g) Details of your family who were living with you?   Yes (551) A   h)
                                                      No   4   i)

IF YES AT g)
h) How did you feel about those questions?

INTERVIEWER RATING   +3   +2   +1   0   -1   -2   -3

i) Details of your partner and whether and why he was living elsewhere?   Yes (552) A   h)
                                                                          No   4   Q.32

IF YES AT i)
j) How did you feel about those questions?

INTERVIEWER RATING   +3   +2   +1   0   -1   -2   -3

- 25 -

		Col./ Code	Skip to
32.a)	When you claimed you would have had to give some <u>evidence</u> of your financial circumstances such as your earnings, your income etc. Did you have any strong feelings one way or the other about this? Yes	(553) A	b)
	No	4	c)
	IF YES AT a) b) How did you feel about it?		
	INTERVIEWER RATING +3 +2 +1 0 -1 -2 -3		
c)	You would also have had to give the name of your (and your husband/ wife/partner's) employer. Did you have strong feelings one way or the other about that? Yes	(554) A	d)
	IF YES AT c) No	4	Q.33
	d) How did you feel about it?		
	INTERVIEWER RATING +3 +2 +1 0 -1 -2 -3		
33.a)	When you applied for FIS, did you have any dealings with officials from the local Social Security office? Yes	(555) A	b)
	No	4	Q.34
	IF YES AT a) b) How did you feel about the way you were treated by the officials?		
	ITNERVIEWER RATING +3 +2 +1 0 -1 -2 -3		
34.	Did you go to the social security office for any reason? Yes	(556) A	b)
	IF YES AT a) No	4	Q.35
	b) How did you feel about that?		
	INTERVIEWER RATING +3 +2 +1 0 -1 -2 -3	(557)	
	c) Were there other people there waiting to be seen? Yes	A	d)
	IF YES AT c) No	4	Q.35
	d) How did you feel about being in their company?		
	INTERVIEWER RATING +3 +2 +1 0 -1 -2 -3		

			Col./Code	Skip to
	ASK CLAIMANTS WHOSE CLAIM WAS SUCCESSFUL (CODE 1 AT Q.5a or 8a) OTHERS SKIP TO Q.36		(558-59)	
35.a)	When you started to receive your _____ (MAIN BENEFIT) (the last time) how much did you get each week?			
		£25 or more	01	
		£20 up to £25	02	
		£15 up to £20	03	
		£10 up to £15	04	
		£8 up to £10	05	
		£6 up to £8	06	
		£5 up to £6	07	
		£4 up to £5	08	
		£3 up to £4	09	
		£2 up to £3	10	
		Less than £2	11	
		Don't know/can't remember	12	
b)	Was this more, less or about the same as you expected?		(560)	
		More	1	Q.36
		Less	2	c)
		Same	3	Q.36
		Didn't know what to expect	4	c)
	IF LESS OR DIDN'T KNOW		(561)	
	c) Did you feel it was worthwhile making the claim for this amount or not?	Yes, worthwhile	1	Q.36
		No, not worthwhile	2	
36.	ALL CLAIMANTS Thinking back over the application procedure, was there anything about it that was better than you expected?		(562)	
		Yes	1	b)
		No	2	Q.37
	IF YES AT a) b) What was it that you found better than expected? PROBE FULLY AND RECORD VERBATIM.			

			Col./ Code	Skip to
37.a)	And thinking back, was there anything that you particularly disliked?		(563)	
		Yes	1	b)
		No	2	c)
	IF YES AT a) b) What was it that you disliked? PROBE FULLY AND RECORD VERBATIM.			
c)	Was there anything about the application procedure that nearly put you off making a claim at all?		(564)	
		Yes	1	d)
		No	2	Q.76
	IF YES AT c) d) What was it that nearly put you off? PROBE FULLY AND RECORD VERBATIM.			
	e) And what was it that made you decide to continue with the claim? PROBE FULLY AND RECORD VERBATIM.			
	NOW SKIP TO Q.76			

NON CLAIMANTS

38. We recently sent you a letter telling you about benefits you might be able to claim. It said that you might be eligible for _____(MAIN BENEFIT) and _____(SECOND BENEFIT) and _____(THIRD BENEFIT). Do you remember receiving the letter?

		Col./Code	Skip-to
		(565)	
Yes		1	b)
No		2	d)
Not sure		3	

IF YES AT a)
b) How did you feel about the possibility of being eligible for this/these benefit(s).
PROBE FULLY AND RECORD VERBATIM

c) Had you heard of _____(MAIN BENEFIT) before you received our letter?

		(566)	
Yes		1	e)
No		2	Q.39

IF NO AT a)
d) Have you heard of _____(MAIN BENEFIT)?

		(567)	
Yes		1	e)
No		2	Q.40

IF YES AT c) OR d)
e) Do you know anyone who receives _____(MAIN BENEFIT)?

		(568)	
Yes		1	f)
No		2	

f) For what kinds of circumstances do you think _____ (MAIN BENEFIT) is intended?

ALL NON-CLAIMANTS

39. Have you (or your husband/wife/partner) seen or heard anything about _____ (MAIN BENEFIT)?
Have you ... READ OUT ...

	Yes	No	Col./Code	Skip to
seen or heard anything on the radio or TV	1	2	(569)	
read anything in a newspaper or magazine	1	2	(570)	
read a booklet or leaflet about the benefit	1	2	(571)	
read some GLC information about the benefit put through your door	1	2	(572)	
seen a notice or poster about the benefit	1	2	(573)	
or seen or heard anything else	1	2	(574)	

(SPECIFY) _____

_____

(575-80) Blank
(601-06) Repeat
(607-08) Card 06

IF YES TO ANY AT a)   IF NO TO ALL SKIP TO Q.40   (609)

b) Did (any of) the things you saw or heard make you think about applying?

Yes	1	c)
No	2	d)

IF YES AT b)
c) What made you think about it?
RECORD SPECIFIC DETAILS OF INFORMATION SOURCE

d) Did (any of) the things you saw or heard put you off the idea of applying?

		(610)	
Yes		1	e)
No		2	Q.40

IF YES AT d)
e) What put you off?
RECORD SPECIFIC DETAILS OF INFORMATION SOURCE

f) Why did this put you off? PROBE FULLY AND RECORD VERBATIM.

			Col./ Code	Skip to
40.a)	ALL NON-CLAIMANTS Have you or (your husband/wife/partner) talked to any of your relatives about the possibility of making a claim for _____ (MAIN BENEFIT)? I mean apart from relatives who live with you?	Yes No	(611) 1 2	b) Q.41

IF YES AT (a)
b) Which relatives did you talk to about it?

ENTER RELATIONSHIP TO RESPONDENT

FOR EACH ASK:
c) How did _____ (REL) feel about you claiming _____ (MAIN BENEFIT)? Do you think he/she generally approved or disapproved?

		(612) (613)	(617) (618)	(622) (623)	(627) (628)
	Approved	1 d)	1 d)	1 d)	1 d)
	Disapproved	2 e)	2 e)	2 e)	2 e)
	No feelings expressed	3 d)&e)	3 d)&e)	3 d)&e)	3 d)&e)

IF CODES 1 OR 3 AT c)
d) Has _____ (REL) encouraged you to make a claim or not?

		(614)	(619)	(624)	(629)
	Yes	1	1	1	1
	No	2 f)	2 f)	2 f)	2 f)
	Can't say	3	3	3	3

IF CODES 2 OR 3 AT c)
e) Has _____ (REL) put you off the idea of making a claim or not?

		(615)	(620)	(625)	(630)
	Yes	1	1	1	1
	No	2 f)	2 f)	2 f)	2 f)
	Can't say	3	3	3	3

f) How much do _____ (RELATIVES'S) views about this matter to you. Do they matter ... READ OUT ...

		(616)	(621)	(626)	(631)
	a great deal	1	1	1	1
	quite a lot	2	2	2	2
	a little	3	3	3	3
	not very much	4	4	4	4
	not at all	5	5	5	5

- 31 -

				Col./ Code	Skip to

ALL NON-CLAIMANTS

41.a) Do you have any (other) relatives you are close to?
DO NOT INCLUDE HOUSEHOLD MEMBERS.

(632)
Yes 1 b)
No 2 Q.42

IF YES AT a)
b) Which other relatives are you close to?

ENTER RELATIONSHIP TO RESPONDENT

FOR EACH ASK

c) How would ____(REL) feel about you claiming ____(MAIN BENEFIT). Do you think he/she would generally approve or disapprove?

d) How much does ____(REL'S) views matter to you. Do they matter ... READ OUT ...

e) If you were thinking of applying for ____(MAIN BENEFIT) would you talk it over with ____(REL) or not?

	(633) (634)	(637) (638)	(641) (642)	(645) (646)
Approve	1	1	1	1
Disapprove	2	2	2	2
Don't know	3	3	3	3
	(635)	(639)	(643)	(647)
a great deal	1	1	1	1
quite a lot	2	2	2	2
a little	3	3	3	3
not very much	4	4	4	4
or not at all	5	5	5	5
	(636)	(640)	(644)	(648)
Yes	1	1	1	1
No	2	2	2	2
Wouldn't think about claiming	3	3	3	3

						Col./ Code	Skip to
42.a)	ALL NON-CLAIMANTS Have you (or your husband/wife/partner) talked to any friends or neighbours you are close to about the possibility of making a claim for _____ (MAIN BENEFIT)?				Yes No	(649) 1 2	b) Q.43

b) Which friends have you talked to about it?

	ENTER IDENTIFIER				
	FOR EACH ASK:				
	c) How did _____ (FRIEND) feel about you claiming _____ (MAIN BENEFIT)? Do you think he/she generally approved or disapproved?	(650) (651)	(655) (656)	(660) (661)	(665) (666)
	Approved	1 d)	1 d)	1 d)	1 d)
	Disapproved	2 e)	2 e)	2 e)	2 e)
	No feelings expressed	3 d)&e)	3 d)&e)	3 d)&e)	3 d)&e)
	IF CODES 1 OR 3 AT c) d) Has _____ (FRIEND) encouraged you to make a claim or not?	(652)	(657)	(662)	(667)
	Yes	1	1	1	1
	No	2 f)	2 f)	2 f)	2 f)
	Can't say	3	3	3	3
	IF CODES 2 OR 3 AT c) e) Have _____ (FRIEND) put you off the idea of making a claim or not?	(653)	(658)	(663)	(668)
	Yes	1	1	1	1
	No	2 f)	2 f)	2 f)	2 f)
	Can't say	3	3	3	3
	ALL f) How much do _____ (FRIEND'S) views matter to you. Do they matter ... READ OUT ...	(654)	(659)	(664)	(669)
	a great deal	1	1	1	1
	quite a lot	2	2	2	2
	a little	3	3	3	3
	not very much	4	4	4	4
	or not at all	5	5	5	5

			Col./Code	Skip to
43.	Do you have any (other) friends or neighbours you are close to?		(670)	
		Yes	1	b)
		No	2	See Q44

IF YES AT a)
b) Which friends or neighbours are you close to?

ENTER IDENTIFIER				
FOR EACH ASK				
e) How would _____ (FRIEND) feel about you claiming _____ (MAIN BENEFIT).	(671)	(709)	(713)	(717)
Do you think he/she would generally approve or disapprove?	(672)	(710)	(714)	(718)
Approve	1	1	1	1
Disapprove	2	2	2	2
Don't know	3	3	3	3
f) How much does _____ (FRIEND) views matter to you. Do they matter... READ OUT ...	(673)	(711)	(715)	(719)
a great deal	1	1	1	1
quite a lot	2	2	2	2
a little	3	3	3	3
not very much	4	4	4	4
or not at all	5	5	5	5
g) If you were thinking of applying for _____ (MAIN BENEFIT), would you talk it over with _____ (FRIEND) or not?	(674)	(712)	(716)	(720)
Yes	1	1	1	1
No	2	2	2	2
Wouldn't think of applying	3	3	3	3

(675-80) Blank
(701-06) Repeat
(707-08) CARD 07

		Col./ Code	Skip to
	ALL NON-CLAIMANTS WHO HAVE MENTIONED CLOSE FRIENDS OR RELATIVES		
	OTHERS SKIP TO Q.45		
44.a)	If you decided to claim _____ (MAIN BENEFIT), are there any relatives or friends you've mentioned who you would not tell?	(721)	
	Yes	1	b)
	No	2	Q.45
	Would not claim	3	
	IF YES AT a)	(722)	
	b) Which relatives or friends are these? ENTER RELATIONSHIP OR IDENTIFIER	(723)	
		(724)	
	ALL NON-CLAIMANTS		
45.a)	Have you or (your husband/wife/partner) talked to any of the following people about making a claim for _____ (MAIN BENEFIT)?		
	READ OUT IN TURN ...		
	A housing officer, social worker or any other official, 1 2	(725)	
	Someone at the Citizens Advice Bureau or Centreprise, 1 2	(726)	
	Someone on the GLC benefit bus, 1 2	(727)	
	Or anyone else you've not mentioned so far (SPECIFY) 1 2	(728)	
	IF YES TO ANY AT a) IF NO TO ALL AT a) SKIP TO Q.46	(729)	
	b) Did (any of) the people you talked to encourage you to make a claim? Yes	1	c)
	No	2	d)
	IF YES AT b) c) Who encouraged you to claim? ENTER ROLE/ORGANISATION		
	d) Did (any of) the people you talked to put you off the idea of making a claim? Yes	(730) 1	e)
	No	2	Q.46
	IF YES AT d) e) Who put you off the idea? ENTER RELATIONSHIP OR ROLE/ORGANISATION		
	f) Why did they put you off? PROBE FULLY AND RECORD VERBATIM.		

- 34 -

				Col./ Code	Skip to
46. a)	ALL NON CLAIMANTS Have you made any enquiries about _____ (MAIN BENEFIT) at the local Social Security Office or the rebates office?		Yes No	(731) 1 2	b) Q.48
	IF YES AT a) b) When did you make these enquires? Was it ... READ OUT ...		Before Christmas After Christmas (Can't remember)	(732) 1 2 3	c) Q.47
	c) Can you remember approximately which month it was? ENTER MONTH _____		Can't remember	(733-34) 09	
47.a)	IF MADE ENQUIRIES (CODE 1 AT Q.46.a) Did you talk to any of the staff at the benefit office about your claim or make an appointment to see someone?		Yes, talked to staff Yes, made an appointment No	(735) 1 2 3	d) b) Q.48
	IF MADE APPOINTMENT b) Did you have your appointment?		Yes No	(736) 1 2	d) c)
	IF NO AT b) c) Why was that?		SKIP TO Q.48		
	IF TALKED TO STAFF/HAD APPOINTMENT d) Did the staff at the benefit office advise you to make a claim or not?		Yes, advised to make claim Not advised to make claim Don't know	(737) 1 2 3	Q.48 e)
	IF NO, OR DON'T KNOW AT d) e) What did the staff at the benefit office tell you?				

			Col./ Code	Skip to

48.a) (Can I just check) Have you obtained a claim form for _____ (MAIN BENEFIT)?

Yes	(738) 1	
No	2	SEE Q.49
Can't remember	3	

IF YES AT a)
b) Did you fill in the claim form?

	(739)	
Yes	1	d)
No	2	c)
Can't remember	3	

IF NO AT b)
c) Why did you not fill in the claim form?

SKIP TO Q.50

IF YES AT b)
d) Did you take or send the form to the benefit office?

	(740)	
Yes	1	e)
No	2	f)

IF YES AT d)
e) What happened after you sent your claim form in?

SKIP TO Q.50

IF NO AT d)
f) Why did you not send the claim form in?

SKIP TO Q.50

		Col./ Code	Skip to

IF NOT MADE ANY ENQUIRIES (CODE 2 AT Q.46a)   OTHERS SKIP TO Q.50

49.a) Have you (or your husband/wife/partner) thought about applying for _____ (MAIN BENEFIT) since we last saw you in _____ (INT. MONTH)?

(741)
- Yes — 1 — Q.50
- No — 2 — b)

IF NO AT a)
b) When you received our letter telling you you might be able to claim _____ (MAIN BENEFIT), did you think about applying at all or did you just dismiss the idea?

(742)
- Thought to some extent — 1 — c)
- Dismissed idea — 2 ⎫
- Other (SPECIFY) _____ — 3 ⎭ d)
  _____
- Didn't receive letter — 4 — Q.53

IF THOUGHT TO SOME EXTENT (CODE 1 AT b)
c) How seriously did you think about it at that time. Did you think ...

(743)
- very seriously — 1 ⎫
- quite seriously — 2 ⎬ Q.52
- or not very seriously about it — 3 ⎪
- (Can't say) — 4 ⎭

IF DISMISSED IDEA (CODE 2 AT b)
d) Why did you dismiss the idea of applying?
PROBE FULLY AND RECORD VERBATIM

NOW SKIP TO Q.53

	IF THOUGHT OR MADE ENQUIRIES ABOUT A CLAIM (CODE 1 AT Q.46a OR 49a)	Col./ Code	Skip to
50.a)	How seriously have you (or your husband/wife/partner) thought about applying for _____ (MAIN BENEFIT). Have you thought about it ... READ OUT ...	(744)	
	very seriously	1	
	quite seriously	2	b)
	or not very seriously	3	
	(Can't say)	4	
b)	When did you think about the idea of applying? Was it ...	(745)	
	before Christmas	1	Q.51
	or after Christmas	2	
	(Can't say)	3	c)
	IF AFTER CHRISTMAS (CODE 2 AT b)	(746)	
c)	Was it before or after you received our letter about benefits you might be able to claim?		
	Before	1	
	After	2	Q.51
	Can't say	3	

	IF THOUGHT OR MADE ENQUIRIES ABOUT A CLAIM (CODE 1 AT Q.46a) OR 49.a)		
51.a)	Thinking back, what was it that made you think about the idea of applying for _____ (MAIN BENEFIT)? PROBE FULLY AND RECORD VERBATIM.		
b)	Did anything particular happen that made you consider it?	(747)	
	Yes	1	c)
	No	2	Q.52
	Can't remember	3	
	IF YES AT b) c) What was it that happened?		

			Col./ Code	Skip to
52.a)	Have you decided ... READ OUT ...		(748)	
	... to make a claim		1	b)
	not to make a claim		2	c)
	or are you still thinking about it?		3	d)
	(Can't say)		4	

IF DECIDED TO MAKE CLAIM (CODE 1 AT a)
b) What has made you decide to make a claim?
   PROBE FULLY AND RECORD VERBATIM

SKIP TO Q.53

IF DECIDED NOT TO CLAIM (CODE 2 AT a)
c) Why have you decided not to make a claim?
   PROBE FULLY AND RECORD VERBATIM

SKIP TO Q.53

IF STILL THINKING OR CAN'T SAY (CODES 3 OR 4 AT a)
d) What is it that makes you uncertain about making a claim?
   PROBE FULLY AND RECORD VERBATIM

		Col./ Code	Skip to
53.a)	ALL NON-CLAIMANTS Has anything at all put you off the idea of applying for _____ (MAIN BENEFIT)? 　　　　　　　　　　　　　　　Yes 　　　　　　　　　　　　　　　No 　　　　　　　　　　　　　　Can't say	(749) 1 2 3	}Q.54
b)	IF YES AT a) What has put you off the idea? 　PROBE FULLY AND RECORD VERBATIM		
54.a)	I'd like you to think about the first thing you would have to do if you decided to apply for _____ (MAIN BENEFIT). What do you imagine that would be? 　　　　　　　　　　　Don't know/Can't say	9	SEE INTER-VIEWER CHECK BELOW
b)	How would you feel about doing that? INTERVIEWER RATING　　+3　　+2　　+1　　0　　-1　　-2　　-3		
	INTERVIEWER CHECK 　　　MAIN BENEFIT IS SUPPLEMENTARY BENEFIT 　　　MAIN BENEFIT IS HOUSING BENEFIT 　　　MAIN BENEFIT IS FAMILY INCOME SUPPLEMENT	(750) 1 2 3	Q.55 Q.62 Q.67

- 41 -

		Col./Code	Skip to

MAIN BENEFIT: SUPPLEMENTARY BENEFIT

55. I'd like to spend a few minutes talking about the application procedure for supplementary benefit. For each part of the procedure I mention I would like you to tell me how you would feel about it.

a) If you claimed you would have to apply to the Social Security Office to verify that you were eligible. Would you have any strong feelings one way or the other about applying to the Social Security Office

    Yes   (751) A   b)
    No   4   See Q56

IF YES AT a)
b) How would you feel about it?

INTERVIEWER RATING   +3   +2   +1   0   -1   -2   -3

PENSIONERS ONLY (RESPONDENT OR SPOUSE 65/60 OR OVER)
    NON-PENSIONERS SEE Q.57

56. a) If you claimed you would have to have an interview with a Social Security official. Would you have any strong feelings about that one way or the other?

    Yes   (752) A   b)
    No   4   c)

IF YES AT a)
b) How would you feel about it?

INTERVIEWER RATING   +3   +2   +1   0   -1   -2   -3

c) You could have an interview either here in your home or you could go to the local social security office. Which do you think you would prefer?

    At home   (753) 1   d)
    At Social Security office   2
    Can't say   3   Q.59

d) Would you have any strong feelings either way about having the interview at home/at the social security office?

    Yes   (754) A   e)
    No   4   Q.59

e) How would you feel about having the interview at home/ at the social security office?

INTERVIEWER RATING   +3   +2   +1   0   -1   -2   -3   → Q.59

		Col./ Code	Skip to
	NON-PENSIONERS (UNEMPLOYED)		
	IF RESPONDENT OR SPOUSE UNEMPLOYED (CODE 3 ON ACTIVITY STATUS) OTHERS SKIP TO Q58		
57.a)	If you applied you would have to go to the Unemployment Benefit Office to get a claim form. Would you have any strong feelings one way or the other about that? Yes No	(755) A 4	b) Q.58
	IF YES AT a) b) How would you feel about it?		
	INTERVIEWER RATING +3 +2 +1 0 -1 -2 -3		
58.a)	ALL NON-PENSIONERS If you decided to apply you would have to fill in a claim form. Would you have any strong feelings one way or the other about that? Yes No	(756) A 4	b) c)
	IF YES AT a) b) How would you feel about that?		
	INTERVIEWER RATING +3 +2 +1 0 -1 -2 -3		
c)	If you applied you might have to have an interview with an official from the social security office. Would you have any strong feelings one way or the other about that? Yes No	(757) A 4	d) e)
	IF YES AT c) d) How would you feel about that?		
	INTERVIEWER RATING +3 +2 +1 0 -1 -2 -3	(758)	
e)	How would you feel about going to the social security office for an interview?		
	INTERVIEWER RATING +3 +2 +1 0 -1 -2 -3		

- 43 -

ALL SUPPLEMENTARY BENEFIT NON CLAIMANTS

59. Whether you completed a claim form or had an interview you would have to answer quite a few questions. I'd like to know how you would feel about having to answer some of these questions.

Would you feel strongly one way or the other about questions on ...

		Col./Code	Skip to
a) Your weekly income, its amount and where it comes from?	Yes / No	(759) A / 4	b) / c)

IF YES AT a)
b) How would you feel about those questions?

+3   +2   +1   0   -1   -2   -3

		Col./Code	Skip to
c) Your savings, their amount and where you have them saved?	Yes / No	(760) A / 4	d) / e)

IF YES AT c)
d) How would you feel about those questions?

+3   +2   +1   0   -1   -2   -3

		Col./Code	Skip to
e) Your health and the health of those living with you?	Yes / No	(761) A / 4	f) / g)

IF YES AT e)
f) How would you feel about those questions?

+3   +2   +1   0   -1   -2   -3

		Col./Code	Skip to
g) How much rent or mortgage you pay and who you pay it to?	Yes / No	(762) A / 4	h) / i)

IF YES AT g)
h) How would you feel about those questions?

+3   +2   +1   0   -1   -2   -3

		Col./Code	Skip to
i) Your family, whether you get any income from them and how much the income amounts to?	Yes / No	(763) A / 4	j) / Q.60

IF YES AT h)
j) How would you feel about those questions?

+3   +2   +1   0   -1   -2   -3

- 44 -

			Col./Code	Skip to
	ALL SUPPLEMENTARY BENEFIT CLAIMANTS			
60.	If you claimed you would have to give some <u>evidence</u> of your financial circumstances such as your <u>savings</u>, your rent book, your order book, etc. Would you have any strong feelings one way or the other about this?	Yes No	(764) 1 2	b) Q.61

IF YES AT a)
b) How would you feel about it?

INTERVIEWER RATING   +3   +2   +1   0   -1   -2   -3

61.a)	Have you ever visited the local social security office?	Yes No Can't remember	(765) 1 2 3	b) d)
	IF YES AT a) b) Were there other people there waiting to be seen?	Yes No	(766) A 9	c) d)

IF YES AT b)
c) How did you feel about being in their company?

INTERVIEWER RATING   +3   +2   +1   0   -1   -2   -3   → Q.71

IF NO AT a) OR b)
d) I'd like you to think for a minute about the social security office and the other people who might be there. How would you feel about being in their company?

INTERVIEWER RATING   +3   +2   +1   0   -1   -2   -3   → Q.71

	MAIN BENEFIT : HOUSING BENEFIT		Col./ Code	Skip to
62.	I'd like to spend a few minutes talking about the application procedure for rent or rate rebates. For each part of the procedure I mention I would like you to tell me how you would feel about it.			
	If you claimed you would have to apply to the Council's rebate office to verify that you were eligible. Would you have any strong feelings one way or the other about applying to the rebate offfice?	Yes No	(767) A 4	b) c)
	IF YES AT a) b) How would you feel about it.			
	INTERVIEWER RATING +3 +2 +1 0 -1 -2 -3			
c)	You would also have to fill in a claim form. Would you have any strong feelings one way or the other about filling in a claim form?	Yes No	(768) A 4	d) Q.63
	IF YES AT c) d) How would you feel about it.			
	INTERVIEWER RATING +3 +2 +1 0 -1 -2 -3			

			Col./ Code	Skip to

63. When you completed the claim form you would have to answer quite a few questions. I'd like to know how you would feel about having to answer those questions. Would you feel strongly one way or the other about the questions on ... READ OUT ...

a)	Your weekly income, it's amounts and where it comes from?	Yes	(769) A	b)
		No	4	c)

IF YES AT a)
b) How would you feel about these questions?

INTERVIEWER RATING   +3   +2   +1   0   -1   -2   -3

c)	Your savings and the amount of interest you receive	Yes	(770) A	d)
		No	4	e)

IF YES AT c)
d) How would you feel about those questions?

INTERVIEWER RATING   +3   +2   +1   0   -1   -2   -3

e)	Details of your family and other people living with you	Yes	(771) A	f)
		No	4	g)

IF YES AT e)
f) How would you feel about those questions?

INTERVIEWER RATING   +3   +2   +1   0   -1   -2   -3

g)	Your rates, rent and what it covers?	Yes	(772) A	h)
		No	4	Q.64

IF YES AT g)
h) How would you feel about those questions?

INTERVIEWER RATING   +3   +2   +1   0   -1   -2   -3

			Col./ Code	Skip to
64.a)	ALL HOUSING BENEFIT NON-CLAIMANTS If you claimed you would have to give some <u>evidence</u> of your financial circumstances such as your rent or rates, your income, etc. Would you have any strong feelings one way or the other about this? <u>IF YES AT a)</u> b) How would you feel about it?	Yes No	(773) A 4	b) Q.65
	INTERVIEWER RATING +3 +2 +1 0 -1 -2 -3			
65.a)	<u>IF RESPONDENT OR SPOUSE EMPLOYED</u> OTHERS SKIP TO Q.66 If you applied you would have to give the name of your (and your husband/wife/partner's) employer. Would you have any strong feelings one way or the other about that? <u>IF YES AT a)</u> b) How would you feel about it?	Yes No	(774) A 4	b) Q.66
	INTERVIEWER RATING +3 +2 +1 0 -1 -2 -3			
66.a)	Have you ever visited the council's rebate office for any reason?	Yes No Can't remember	(775) 1 2 3	b) d) d)
	<u>IF YES AT a)</u> b) Were there other people there waiting to be seen?	Yes No	(776) A 9	c) d)
	<u>IF YES AT b)</u> c) How did you feel about being in their company?			
	INTERVIEWER RATING +3 +2 +1 0 -1 -2 -3			→ Q.71
	<u>IF NO AT a) OR b)</u> d) I'd like you to think for a minute about the rebate office and the other people who might be there. How would you feel about being in their company?		(777)	
	INTERVIEWER RATING +3 +2 +1 0 -1 -2 -3			→ Q.71

- 48 -

		Col./ Code	Skip to

MAIN BENEFIT : FAMILY INCOME SUPPLEMENT

67. I'd like to spend a few minutes talking about the application procedure for Family Income Supplement. For each part of the procedure I mention I would like you to tell me how you would feel about it.

(778)

a) If you claimed you would have to apply to the DHSS to verify that you were eligible. Would you have any strong feelings one way or the other about applying to the DHSS?

Yes — A — b)
No — 4 — c)

IF YES AT a)
b) How would you feel about it?

INTERVIEWER RATING   +3   +2   +1   0   -1   -2   -3

(779)

c) You would also have to fill in a claim form. Would you have any strong feelings one way or the other about filling in the claim form?

Yes — A — d)
No — 4 — e)

IF YES AT c)
d) How would you feel about it?

INTERVIEWER RATING   +3   +2   +1   0   -1   -2   -3

(780)

e) Your claim would be dealt with by a DHSS office in Blackpool? Would you have any strong feelings one way or the other about this?

Yes — A
No — 4

IF YES AT a)
f) How would you feel about it?

INTERVIEWER RATING   +3   +2   +1   0   -1   -2   -3

(801-06) Repeat
(807-08) Card 08

		Col./ Code	Skip to
68.	When you completed the claim form you would have to answer quite a few questions. I'd like to know how you would feel about having to answer those questions. Would you feel strongly one way or the other about the questions on ... READ OUT ...	(809)	
a)	Your earnings from employment? Yes	A	b)
	No	4	c)
	IF YES AT a) b) How would you feel about those questions?		
	INTERVIEWER RATING +3 +2 +1 0 -1 -2 -3	(810)	
c)	Your savings and the amount of interest you receive? Yes	A	d)
	No	4	e)
	IF YES AT c) d) How would you feel about those questions?		
	INTERVIEWER RATING +3 +2 +1 0 -1 -2 -3	(811)	
e)	Your other sources of income such as benefits, maintenance, income from lodgers, etc. Yes	A	f)
	No	4	g)
	IF YES AT e) f) How would you feel about those questions?		
	INTERVIEWER RATING +3 +2 +1 0 -1 -2 -3	(812)	
g)	Details of your family who were living with you? Yes	A	h)
	No	4	i)
	IF YES AT g) h) How would you feel about those questions?		
	INTERVIEWER RATING +3 +2 +1 0 -1 -2 -3	(813)	
i)	Details of your partner and whether and why he was living elsewhere? Yes	A	j)
	No	4	Q.69
	IF YES AT i) j) How would you feel about those questions?		
	INTERVIEWER RATING +3 +2 +1 0 -1 -2 -3		Q.69

145

			Col./Code	Skip to
69.a)	If you claimed you would have to give some evidence of your financial circumstances such as your earnings, your income etc. Would you have any strong feelings one way or the other about this?	Yes	(814) A	b)
		No	4	c)
	IF YES AT a) b) How would you feel about it?			
	INTERVIEWER RATING +3 +2 +1 0 -1 -2 -3			
c)	If you applied you would have to give the name of your (and your husband/wife/partner's) employer. Would you have any strong feelings one way or the other about that?	Yes	(815) A	d)
		No	4	Q.70
	IF YES AT c) d) How would you feel about it?			
	INTERVIEWER RATING +3 +2 +1 0 -1 -2 -3			
70.	Have you ever visited the local social security office?	Yes	(816) 1	b)
		No	2	d)
		Can't remember	3	d)
	IF YES AT a) b) Were there other people there waiting to be seen?	Yes	(817) A	c)
		No	9	d)
	IF YES AT b) c) How did you feel about being in their company?			
	INTERVIEWER RATING +3 +2 +1 0 -1 -2 -3		(818)	
	IF NO AT a) or b) d) I'd like you to think for a minute about the social security office and the other people who might be there. How would you feel about being in their company?			
	INTERVIEWER RATING +3 +2 +1 0 -1 -2 -3			

- 51 -

		Col./Code	Skip to
71.a)	ALL NON-CLAIMANTS (Can I just check) Have you ever had any dealings with an official from a local social security office? Yes No Can't remember	(819) 1 2 3	Q.72 b)
b)	IF NO/CAN'T REMEMBER (CODES 2 OR 3) AT a) Have you ever had any dealings with an official from the Council's rebate office? Yes No Can't remember	(820) 1 2 3	Q.72 c)
c)	IF NO/CAN'T REMEMBER (CODES 2 OR 3) AT b) Have you ever had any dealings with any other officials such as tax officers, rent or rates officials, gas or electricity officials? Yes No Can't remember	(821) 1 2 3	Q.72 Q.73
72.a)	IF HAS HAD ANY DEALINGS WITH OFFICIALS (CODE 1 AT Q.71a), b) or c) In general, how do you feel about the way you have been treated by officials in the past? INTERVIEWER RATING +3 +2 +1 0 -1 -2 -3	(822)	
b)	If you decided to apply for (MAIN BENEFIT), how likely do you think it is that you would be treated in the same way? Would you say it is ... very likely quite likely not very likely or not at all likely	(823) 1 2 3 4	Q.74
73.	IF NO DEALINGS WITH OFFICIALS How do you think you would feel about the way officials might treat you, if you applied for _____ (MAIN BENEFIT) INTERVIEWER RATING +3 +2 +1 0 -1 -2 -3	(824)	Q.74

– 52 –

			Col./Code	Skip to
74.a)	ALL NON CLAIMANTS One of the things that might influence your decision to apply for _____ (MAIN BENEFIT) is how much you would get. Looking at this card, how much do you think it might be. SHOW CARD A.		(825-26)	
		£25 or more	01	
		£20 up to £25	02	
		£15 up to £20	03	
		£10 up to £15	04	
		£8 up to £10	05	
		£6 up to £8	06	
		£5 up to £6	07	
		£4 up to £5	08	
		£2 up to £4	09	
		Under £2	10	
		Can't say/don't know	11	
		Nothing/Wouldn't get it	12	
b)	And what is the minimum amount that would make a claim worthwhile?		(827-28)	
		£25 or more	01	
		£20 up to £25	02	
		£15 up to £20	03	
		£10 up to £15	04	
		£8 up to £10	05	
		£6 up to £8	06	
		£5 up to £6	07	
		£4 up to £5	08	
		£2 up to £4	09	
		Under £2	10	
		Can't say/don't know	11	
		Would not claim whatever the amount	12	
75.a)	Thinking generally about the claiming procedure for _____ (MAIN BENEFIT) is there anything about it that might put you off making a claim?		(829)	
		Yes	1	b)
		No	2	Q.76
		Can't say	3	
	IF YES AT a) b) What do you think might put you off?			

148

		Col./ Code	Skip to
	ASK ALL (CLAIMANTS AND NON-CLAIMANTS)		
76.a)	In general, do you feel _____ (MAIN BENEFIT) is a right or a charity. SHOW CARD B Please look at this card and tell me which statement best describes your feelings?	(830)	
	It's very definitely a right	1	
	It's more a right than a charity	2	
	It's a fairly even mixture of both	3	
	It's more a charity than a right	4	
	It's very definitely a charity	5	
b)	Does it matter to you whether it is a right or a charity? Yes	(831) 1	c)
	No	2	} Q.77
	Can't say	3	
	IF YES AT b) c) How much does it matter to you whether it is a right or a charity. Does it matter ... READ OUT ...	(832)	
	a great deal	1	
	quite a lot	2	
	or just a little	3	
	(Can't say)	4	
77.a)	Do you feel that claiming _____ (MAIN BENEFIT) has/ would affect your financial independence in any way? Yes	(833) 1	b)
	No	2	Q.78
	(Can't say)	3	b)
	IF YES AT a) b) Do you feel it would make/has made you ... READ OUT ...	(834)	
	... more independent	1	
	or less independent	2	
	(Can't say)	3	
	RECORD ANY SPONTANEOUS COMMENTS		

			Col./ Code	Skip to
78.a)	ASK ALL Thinking now about your financial situation generally, how difficult do you find it to manage on your present income, would you say it was ... READ OUT ...		(835)	
		No trouble	1	
		A little difficult	2	
		Pretty hard	3	
		A great struggle	4	
		or almost impossible	5	
b)	Looking at this card, which of the statements best describes your situation? SHOW CARD C		(836)	
		Your income is quite a bit greater than your expenses	1	
		Your income is a little bit greater than your expenses	2	
		Your income just matches your expenses	3	
		Your income is a little bit less than your expenses	4	
		Your income is a bit less than your expenses	5	
c)	And now looking at this card, SHOW CARD D, where would you place yourself on this income ladder?		(837)	
		Rich	1	
		More than enough to live on	2	
		Enough	3	
		Not quite enough	4	
		Hard up	5	
		Really poor	6	

		YES	NO	Don't do it	
d)	In the last few months have you had to cut back on any of the following? READ OUT IN TURN.				
	Going out for entertainment	1	2	3	(838)
	Going to the pub, bingo or cinema	1	2	3	(839)
	Going on holiday	1	2	3	(840)
	Travelling to see relatives	1	2	3	(841)
	Heating	1	2	3	(842)
	Using the phone	1	2	3	(843)
	Clothes or shoes	1	2	3	(844)
	Using electricity as much as you need	1	2	3	(845)
	Smoking (check not for health reasons)	1	2	3	(846)
	Buying meat	1	2	3	(847)
	Buying other food	1	2	3	(848)

			Col./Code	Skip to
79.a)	ASK ALL Do you expect any changes in the next few months that might improve your financial circumstances? Yes No Can't say		(849) 1 2 3	b) c)
b)	IF YES AT a) What changes do you expect?			
c)	And do you expect any changes which might make things worse? Yes No Can't say		(850) 1 2 3	d) Q.80
d)	IF YES AT c) What changes do you expect?			
80.a)	If you needed help financially, would you ever consider asking members of your family to help you out or not? Yes, might consider No		(851) 1 2	b)
b)	If you were to ask them, how willing do you think they would be to help you out? Would they be ... READ OUT ... ... very willing quite willing not very willing not at all willing (Would never ask, so can't say) (Don't know)		(852) 1 2 3 4 5 6	c) Q.81 c)
c)	And how able are they to help you out. Are they ... READ OUT ... very able to help quite able not very able or not able to help at all (Can't say because would never ask)		(853) 1 2 3 4 5	

	ALL NON-CLAIMANTS CLAIMANTS SEE Q.82	Col./ Code	Skip to
81.a)	Thinking back over all the things we've talked about, how likely do you think it is that you will claim _____ (MAIN BENEFIT)? SHOW CARD E. Which of these statements best describes what you think you will do?	(854)	
	Definitely will	1	
	Very likely will	2	
	Probably will, but not certain	3	
	Probably will not, but not certain	4	
	Very likely will not, but there's a slight chance	5	
	Definitely will not	6	
b)	Why do you feel that?		
	IF CODES 1 - 3 AT a) OTHERS SEE Q.82	(855)	
c)	Do you think you might make a claim in the next week or two, or not?		
	Yes	1	SEE Q.82
	No	2	
	Can't say	3	

		Col./ Code	Skip to

IF SECOND BENEFIT LISTED, ASK Q.82.   **OTHERS SKIP TO Q.86**

82.a) When we wrote to you we also mentioned that you might be eligible for _____ (SECOND BENEFIT). Can I check, have you made a claim for _____ (SECOND BENEFIT) since _____ (INT. DATE)?

(856)

                             Yes   1   b)
                             No   2   Q.83

(857)

IF YES AT a)

b) When did you apply. Was it ... READ OUT ...

                      before Christmas   1
                      or after Christmas   2   c)
                      (can't remember)   3   d)

(858-59)

c) Can you remember approximately which month it was?

                    ENTER MONTH _____
                            Can't remember   08   d)

d) Thinking back, what was it that made you decide to apply for _____ (SECOND BENEFIT).

PROBE FULLY AND RECORD VERBATIM.

e) What was the result of your claim. Were you ... READ OUT ...

(860)

                    Given the benefit   1
                Or was your claim turned down   2   Q.84
                        (Not yet heard)   3

			Col./ Code	Skip to
	IF NOT CLAIMED SECOND BENEFIT (CODE 2 AT Q.82a)		(861)	
83.a)	How seriously have you thought about applying for _____ (SECOND BENEFIT). Have you thought about it ... READ OUT ...			
		very seriously	1	
		quite seriously	2	c)
		or not very seriously	3	
		or not at all	4	b)
	IF NOT AT ALL		(862)	
b)	When you received our letter telling you you might be able to claim _____ (SECOND BENEFIT), did you think about applying at all or did you just dismiss the idea?			
		Thought to some extent	1	c)
		Dismissed idea	2	
		Other (SPECIFY) _____	3	e)
	IF THOUGHT AT ALL		(863)	
c)	How likely do you think it is that you will apply for _____ (SECOND BENEFIT)? SHOW CARD E			
		I definitely will	1	
		I very likely will	2	
		I probably will, but am not certain	3	
		I probably won't, but am not certain	4	
		I very likely will not, but there's a slight chance	5	
		I definitely will not	6	
d)	Why do you say that? PROBE FULLY AND RECORD VERBATIM			
		NOW SKIP TO Q.84		
	IF DISMISSED IDEA AT (CODES 2 or 3 AT c)			
e)	Why did you dismiss the idea? PROBE FULLY AND RECORD VERBATIM			

- 59 -

		Col./Code	Skip to

ASK ALL WITH SECOND BENEFIT

84. Is there anything about claiming _____(SECOND BENEFIT) that you feel would be different from _____(MAIN BENEFIT)

(864)

- Yes — 1 — b)
- No — 2 ⎫
- Don't know/Can't say — 3 ⎬ Q.85

IF YES AT a)
b) What do you feel would be different about claiming _____(SECOND BENEFIT)?

c) Would that make it better or worse than claiming _____(MAIN BENEFIT)?

(865)

- Better — 1
- Worse — 2
- Better in some ways, worse in others — 3
- Can't say — 4

85. a) Thinking about _____(MAIN BENEFIT) and _____(SECOND BENEFIT) in general, which would you prefer to claim?

(866)

- Main benefit — 1 ⎫
- Second benefit — 2 ⎬ b)
- Either/don't mind — 3 ⎪
- Neither — 4 ⎭

b) Why do you say that?

- 60 -

		Col./Code	Skip to

86. ASK ALL

When we spoke to you last time, we collected a lot of information about your employment/housing and financial situation. As people's circumstances can change I would just like to check about any changes there may have been.

a) Looking at this card (SHOW CARD F) which category best describes your present position?

(867)

	Code	Skip
Working (full-time)	1	b)
Working (part-time)	2	b)
Government training schemes (e.g. TOPS, YTS, Comm. programme)	3	Q.88
Retired from main occupation but working (F/PT)	4	b)
Unemployed/seeking work	5	
Full-time education	6	
Wholly retired	7	Q.88
Permanently sick/disabled	8	
Housewife/look after a home/a family	9	
Other (SPECIFY) _____	0	

IF WORKING FULL OR PART TIME (CODES 1, 2 OR 4) AT a) (868)

b) Thinking about your present earnings from work, are you normally paid ... READ OUT ...

... weekly,	1
fortnightly,	2
monthly,	3
or for some other period (SPECIFY)	4

_____

c) What was your <u>gross</u> pay last ____ (period at a), that is, your pay including any overtime, tips or bonuses but <u>before</u> any deductions for national insurance, income tax or any other expenses? IF SELF-EMPLOYED: How much did you make <u>before</u> deductions?

(869-73)

£   p

ENTER GROSS PAY FOR PERIOD AT a).
IF VARIES, TAKE AVERAGE LAST MONTH.

d) And, what was your <u>net</u> pay last ____ (period at a), that is, your pay including any overtime, tips or bonuses but AFTER any deductions are made for national insurance, income tax or any other expenses? IF SELF-EMPLOYED: How much did you make <u>after</u> deductions?

(874-78)

£   p

e) Were you doing the same job when we spoke to you last ____ (INT. MONTH)?

(879)

Yes	1	See Q.90
No	2	Q.87

(880)	Blank
(901-06)	Repeat
(907-08)	Card 09

156

		Col./Code	Skip to
	IF DOING DIFFERENT JOB (CODE 2 AT Q.86e)	(909-10)	
87.a)	When did you start your present job? ENTER MONTH: _____		
b)	What is your present job? Job title: .... Brief description of activity:	(911)	
c)	Are you an employee or self-employed? Employee Self-employed	(912) 1 2	
d)	How many hours do you usually work each week, excluding overtime? HOURS PER WEEK IF VARIES, TAKE USUAL	(913-14)	
e)	Do you usually work overtime? Yes No	(915) 1 2	h)
	IF YES AT e)		
f)	About how many hours overtime do you usually work each week? HOURS PER WEEK	(916-17)	
g)	Is that paid or unpaid overtime? Paid Unpaid	(918) 1 2	
h)	How much does it cost you to travel to work each week? (If travels by car, motorcycle or bicycle: approximately how much would it cost you to travel to work each week by public transport?) £ p ENTER AMOUNT (ACCEPT ESTIMATE)	(919-22)	Q.88

			Col./ Code	Skip to
88.a)	Were you working when we spoke to you in _____ (INT. MONTH)		(923)	
		Yes	1	b)
		No	2	Q.89
			(924-25)	
	IF YES			
b)	When did the job you were doing then finish? ENTER _____ MONTH			
			(926)	
c)	Did you register as unemployed when that job finished?	Yes	1	
		No	2	Q.89
			(927)	
89.	Have you had any (other) jobs since _____ (INT. MONTH)?	Yes	1	b)
		No	2	See Q.90
			(928)	
	IF YES AT a)			
b)	What other jobs have you had? Starting with your last job: ... LAST JOB Job title		(929)	
i)	Was it full-time or part time?	Full time	1	
		Part time	2	
			(930-31)	
ii)	When did you start that job? ENTER MONTH		(932-33)	
iii)	And when did that job finish? ENTER MONTH		(934)	
iv)	Did you register as unemployed when that job finished?	Yes	1	
		No	2	
			(935)	
c)	JOB BEFORE LAST JOB Job title		9 (936)	
i)	Was it full-time or part time?	Full time	1	
		Part time	2	
			(937-38)	
ii)	When did you start that job? ENTER MONTH		(939-40)	
iii)	When did that job finish? ENTER MONTH		(941)	
iv)	And did you register as unemployed when that job finished?	Yes	1	SEE Q.90
		No	2	

– 63 –

			Col./Code	Skip to
	IF MARRIED OR LIVING AS MARRIED OTHERS SEE Q.94			
90.a)	Looking at this card again (SHOW CARD F) which category best describes your husband/wife/partner's present position?		(942)	
		Working (full-time)	1	b)
		Working (part-time)	2	b)
		Government training schemes (eg. TOPS, YTS, Comm. programme)	3	Q.92
		Retired from main occupation but working (F/PT)	4	b)
		Unemployed/seeking work	5	
		Full-time education	6	
		Wholly retired	7	Q.92
		Permanently sick/disabled	8	
		Housewife/look after a home/a family	9	
	Other (SPECIFY) _____		0	
	IF WORKING FULL OR PART TIME (CODES 1, 2 OR 4)		(943)	
b)	Thinking about his/her present earnings from work, is he/she normally paid ... READ OUT ...	... weekly,	1	
		fortnightly,	2	
		monthly,	3	
		or for some other period (SPECIFY)	4	
c)	What was his/her gross pay last ____ (period at a), that is, his/her pay including any overtime, tips or bonuses but before any deductions for national insurance, income tax or any other expenses? IF SELF-EMPLOYED: How much did he/she make before deductions?		(944-48)	
	ENTER GROSS PAY FOR PERIOD AT a). IF VARIES, TAKE AVERAGE LAST MONTH	£ p		
		Don't know	99998	
d)	And, what was his/her net pay last ____ (period at a), that is, his/her pay including any overtime, tips or bonuses but AFTER any deductions are made for national insurance, income tax or any other expenses? IF SELF-EMPLOYED: How much did he/she make after deductions?		(949-53)	
	ENTER NET PAY FOR PERIOD AT a). IF VARIES, TAKE AVERAGE LAST MONTH	£ p		
		Don't know	99998	
			(954)	
e)	Was he/she doing the same job when we spoke to you last ____ (INT. MONTH)	Yes	1	SEE Q94
		No	2	Q.91

159

			Col./ Code	Skip to

		IF SPOUSE/PARTNER DOING DIFFERENT JOB (CODE 2 AT Q.90e)	(955-56)	
91.a)		When did your husband/wife/partner start his/her present job? ENTER MONTH: _____		
			(957)	
	b)	What is his/her present job? Job title: .... Brief description of activity:		
			(958)	
	c)	Is he/she an employee or self-employed? Employee Self-employed	1 2	
			(959-60)	
	d)	How many hours does he/she usually work each week, excluding overtime? HOURS PER WEEK IF VARIES, TAKE USUAL		
			(961)	
	e)	Does he/she usually work overtime? Yes No	1 2	h)
		IF YES AT e)	(962-63)	
	f)	About how many hours overtime does he/she work each week? HOURS PER WEEK		
			(964)	
	g)	Is that paid or unpaid overtime? Paid Unpaid	1 2	
	h)	How much does it usually cost him/her to travel to work each week? (If travels by car, motorcycle or bicycle: approximately how much would it cost him/her to travel to work each week by public transport?) £ p ENTER AMOUNT (ACCEPT ESTIMATE)	(965-68)	Q.92

				Col./ Code	Skip to
92.a)	Was your husband/wife/partner working when we spoke to you in _____(INT. MONTH)?		Yes	(969) 1	b)
			No	2	Q.93
	IF YES			(970-71)	
b)	When did the job he/she was doing then finish? ENTER _____ MONTH				
c)	Did he/she register as unemployed when that job finished?		Yes	(972) 1	Q.93
			No	2	
93.a)	Has he/she had any (other) jobs since _____ (INT. MONTH)?		Yes	(973) 1	b)
			No	2	SEE Q94
b)	IF YES AT a) What other jobs has he/she had? Starting with his/her last job: ...			(974)	
	LAST JOB				
	Job Title			(975)	
	i) Was it full-time or part time?	Full time		1	
		Part time		2	
	ii) When did he/she start that job? ENTER MONTH			(976-77)	
	iii) And when did that job finish? ENTER MONTH			(978-79)	
	iv) And did he/she register as unemployed when that job finished?		Yes	(980) 1	
			No	2	
				1001-06	Repeat
c)	JOB BEFORE LAST JOB			1007-08	Card 10
				(1009)	
	Job Title			(1010)	
	i) Was it full-time or part time?	Full time		1	
		Part time		2	
	ii) When did he/she start that job? ENTER MONTH			(1011-12)	
	iii) And when did that job finish? ENTER MONTH			(1013-14)	
	iv) And did he/she register as unemployed when that job finished?		Yes	(1015) 1	SEE Q94
			No	2	

- 66 -

			Col./ Code	Skip to
94.a)	IF HOUSEHOLDER (CLAIM UNIT NO = 1) NON-HOUSEHOLDER SKIP TO Q.102 Can I just check again do you and your household own or rent your accommodation?		(1016)	
		Own	1	Q.96
		Rent	2	Q.95
		Live rent free	3	b)
	IF LIVES RENT FREE (CODE 3 AT a)		(1017)	
	b) Do you pay rates for this accommodation?	Yes	1	Q.97
		No	2	Q.98
95.a)	IF RENTS (CODE 2 AT Q.94a) What is the current rent charged for this accommodation? £ p ENTER AMOUNT CHARGED PER WEEK		(1018-21)	b)
		Don't know	9998	
b)	Does that amount include rates or do you pay the rates directly to the Council?	Rent includes rates	(1022) 1	c)
		Rates paid separately	2	d)
	IF RENT INCLUDES RATES (CODE 1 AT b)		(1023)	
c)	Do you know how much the rates are for this accommodation?	Yes	1	d)
	CHECK RENT BOOK WHERE POSSIBLE	No	2	e)
	IF YES (CODES 1 OR 2 AT c)		(1024-27)	
d)	How much are the rates for this accommodation? £ p ENTER AMOUNT PER WEEK			
	ALL RENTERS			
e)	Does the rent you pay include an amount for gas, electricity, heating, hot water, or any other services?	Yes	(1028) 1	f)
		No	2	g)
	IF YES AT e)		(1029-32)	
f)	How much in total is charged for these services? £ p CHECK RENT BOOK WHERE POSSIBLE ENTER AMOUNT PER WEEK			g)
		Don't know	9998	
	CHECK WITH ALL		(1033-36)	
g)	So (after deducting the rates and other costs), your weekly net rent would be how much? £ p SUBTRACT AMOUNT AT d) AND f) FROM RENT AND ENTER IN BOX CHECK RENT BOOK WHERE POSSIBLE.			Q.98
		Don't know	9998	

162

		Col./ Code	Skip to
96.	IF OWNS (CODE 1 AT Q.94a) How much are your mortgage payments now for this accommodation? I mean the amount you actually pay each month? ENTER AMOUNT PAID PER MONTH £ ⬜⬜⬜ Nothing, owns outright Nothing, paid by person outside household	(1037-39) 000 998	
97.	IF OWNS OR PAYS RATES (CODE 1 AT Q.94a OR Q.94b) How much are the rates now for this accommodation? ENTER AMOUNT £ ⬜⬜⬜ AND PERIOD IT COVERS _____	(1040-43)	
98.	INTERVIEWER CHECK IF AT SAME ADDRESS AS FIRST INTERVIEW (CODE 1 AT Q.1a) IF MOVED (CODE A AT Q.1a) AND NOW RENTS AND NOW LIVES RENT FREE AND NOW OWNS	(1044) 1 2 3 4	Q.102 Q.99 Q.102 Q.100
99.a)	IF MOVED AND RENTS (CODE 2 AT Q.98) Does the rent you pay include water rates? Yes No	(1045) 1 2	b) c)
	IF YES AT a) b) How much is included in your rent for water rates? ENTER AMOUNT PAID EACH WEEK £ ⬜ p ⬜ Not known Rent book checked Rent book not checked	(1046-48) 998 (1049) 1 2	
c)	Does the rent you pay include an amount for a service charge? Yes No	(1050) 1 2	d) Q.101
	IF YES AT c) d) How much of your rent is for a service charge? ENTER AMOUNT PAID EACH WEEK £ ⬜ p ⬜ Not known Rent book checked Rent book not checked	(1051-54) 9998 (1055) 1 2	Q.101

			Col./Code	Skip to
100.a)	**MOVED AND OWNS (CODE 4 AT Q.98)** How much are the water rates for this accommodation? ENTER AMOUNT AND PERIOD IT COVERS		(1056-58) £	
b)	Is your property freehold or leasehold?	Freehold Leasehold	(1059) 1 2	Q.101 c)
	IF LEASEHOLD AT b)		(1060)	
c)	Do you pay ground rent?	Yes No	1 2	d) e)
	IF YES AT c)			
d)	How much ground rent do you pay? £ ___ p ___ per ENTER PERIOD		(1061-67)	
	IF LEASEHOLD		(1068)	
e)	Do you pay service charges?	Yes No	1 2	f) Q.101
	IF YES AT e)			
f)	How much are your service charges? £ ___ p ___ per ENTER PERIOD		(1069-75)	Q.101
101.a)	**ALL MOVERS** Do you sub-let any part of this accommodation to anyone who is not part of this household?	Yes No	(1076) 1 2	b) c)
	IF YES AT a)		(1077-80)	
b)	How much rent in total do you receive from your sub-tenants each week? £ ___ p ___ ENTER TOTAL AMOUNT RECEIVED PER WEEK			c)
			(1101-06) (1107-08)	Repeat CARD 11
c)	How many rooms do you (and your household) have in this house/flat, apart from the bathroom and toilet? EXCLUDE ROOMS USED SOLELY BY SUBTENANTS NUMBER OF ROOMS (Living rooms, bedrooms/kitchen)		(1109) (1110)	
d)	(Can I just check), do you have central heating?	Yes No	1 2	e) Q.102
	IF YES AT d)		(1111)	
e)	Is your central heating ... READ OUT ...	full central heating, partial central heating, or storage heaters?	1 2 3	

- 68 -

164

- 69 -

ASK ALL
102. Finally, could I just check what sources of income you (and your husband/wife/partner have), apart from any earnings from employment.

a) Could you look at this card and tell me if you (or your husband/wife/partner) are receiving any of the benefits or pensions shown, including any I've asked you about before? Any others? SHOW CARD G. ENTER IN (a)

FOR EACH BENEFIT RECEIVED ASK (b) AND (c)

b) Who receives ... (benefit at a))? ENTER IN b)

c) How much do you (does your husband/wife/partner) receive each week from ... (benefit at (a))? ENTER IN c)

(1178-80) Blank
(1201-06) Repeat
(1207-08) CARD 12

		(a)	(b) Respondent	Husband/wife/partner	(c) Amount received each week £ p	
A	Supplementary benefit/pension	1	1	2		(1112-17)
B	Family Income Supplement	2	1	2		(1118-23)
C	Housing Benefit (rent all/rebate/rate rebate)	3	1	2		(1124-29)
D	Child Benefit (incl. one parent addition)	4	1	2		(1130-35)
E	Unemployment Benefit	5	1	2		(1136-41)
F	State Retirement Pension	6	1	2		(1142-47)
G	Sickness Benefit	7	1	2		(1148-53)
H	Child Special Allowance	8	1	2		(1154-59)
I	Widow's Allowance	9	1	2		(1160-65)
J	Widowed mother's allowance	0	1	2		(1166-71)
K	Widow's pension	1	1	2		(1172-77)
L	War widow's pension	2	1	2		(1209-14)
M	Maternity Allowance	3	1	2		(1215-20)
N	Invalidity Benefit/Pension	4	1	2		(1221-26)
O	Non-contributory invalidity benefit	5	1	2		(1227-32)
P	Attendance Allowance	6	1	2		(1233-38)
Q	Mobility Allowance	7	1	2		(1239-44)
R	Industrial Death Pension/Allowance/Benefit	8	1	2		(1245-50)
S	Other war, industrial benefits, pensions, allowances (SPECIFY) _____ _____	9	1	2		(1251-56)
T	Free school meals for your children	0	1	2		(1257-58)
V	Fares to school for your children	1	1	2		(1259-60)
X	NONE OF THESE	2				(1261)

103. Do you (or your husband/wife/partner) have any income from any of the sources on this card? Any others?
SHOW CARD H.   ENTER IN (a)

FOR EACH RECEIVED ASK b)

b) Who receives ... (payment at a)?
c) How much do you (does your husband/wife/partner) receive from .... (payment at b)?
d) What period does that cover?

(1278-80)
(1301-06)
(1307-08)

Blank
Repeat
CARD 13

	(a) CODE ALL THAT APPLY	(b) WHO RECEIVES			(c) AMOUNT RECEIVED £ p	(d) PERIOD	
		Respondent	Husband/wife/partner	Joint Receipt			
Maintenance payments (including affiliation orders/ or court orders)	1	1	2	3		_____	(1262-69)
Interest from savings (e.g. Building Society/Post Office deposit accounts etc.)	2	1	2	3		_____	(1270-77)
Interest from other savings or investments	3	1	2	3		_____	(1309-16)
Payments from endowment or private pension policies	4	1	2	3		_____	(1317-24)
Pensions from former employment (self or spouse)	5	1	2	3		_____	(1326-32)
Foster child allowance	6	1	2	3		_____	(1333-40)
Income from other members of the family (outside of household)	7	1	2	3		_____	(1341-48)
Rents from property or sub-letting	8	1	2	3		_____	(1349-56)
Job release scheme payments	9	1	2	3		_____	(1357-64)
Lodging and travel allowances for Government training schemes e.g. TOP's, YTS, etc.	0	1	2	3		_____	(1365-72)
Income from casual employment	1	1	2	3		_____	(1373-80)
Any other sources of income? (SPCIFY) _____ _____	2	1	2	3		_____	(1409-16)
NONE OF THESE	3						(1417)

(1401-06)
(1407-08)

Repeat
CARD 14

- 71 -

			Col./Code	Skip to
			(1418)	
104.	(Can I just check) do you (or your husband/wife/partner) have savings of £2,500 or more? Yes		1	
	No		2	

105.a) Do you make any regular payments for any of the following items ... READ OUT IN TURN AND RECORD IN COLUMN a)

IF YES AT ANY ITEMS: How much do you pay for ... (RECORD IN COLUMN b)

	(a) Yes No	(b) IF YES: AMOUNT/PERIOD	
Costs of having children looked after whilst you are at work	1 2	£ ___ p ___ per ___ ENTER PERIOD	(1419-25)
Essential domestic help because you (and your husband/wife/partner) are prevented from doing domestic work because of disability or heavy family responsibilities.	1 2	£ ___ p ___ per ___ ENTER PERIOD	(1426-32)
Maintenance payments (for ex-wife and or children)	1 2	£ ___ p ___ per ___ ENTER PERIOD	(1433-39)

106. Is there anything else you would like to add about the benefits we've discussed or about your own circumstances? (1440)

107. There is one final point on which we would like your help. In this follow-up study, we are talking to several hundred people who, like yourself, have been sent a letter telling them about benefits they might be able to claim. In a few months time, we would like to be able to check how many people have made a claim and whether the claim was successful. Rather than come back to everyone again, we would like to be able to check this information with the relevant benefit office. We would only be able to do this, however, if we had the permission of the people we've seen. Would you be willing for us to check this information with ..... social security office (IF SUPPLEMENTARY BENEFIT) ..... housing benefit office (IF HOUSING BENEFIT), the DHSS (if FIS)? (1441)

Respondent signed form 1
Respondent not willing to sign form 2

167

	Col./Code	Skip to
TO BE COMPLETED BY INTERVIEWER		
Time interview ended	(1442-44)	
Length of interview .... MINUTES		
Interviewer name _____ No. ☐☐☐☐	(1445-48)	
Date of interview ___/___/1984	(1449-1552)	

Any comments/observations about the interview:

References

1 ALLISON F. *The non-take up of benefits—the would-be claimant's obstacle course* Unpublished MA Thesis, University of Bath, 1982.

2 BRIGGS E. and REES A. *Supplementary benefit and the consumer* London, Bedford Square Press, 1980.

3 COHEN R. and TARPEY M. *Benefit take-up: a review* London, Islington People's Rights Action Research Project, 1985.

4 CORDEN A. *Taking up a means tested benefit: the process of claiming family income supplement* London, HMSO, 1983.

5 DEPARTMENT OF EMPLOYMENT *New earnings survey 1983, Part E analyses by region and age group* London, HMSO, 1984.

6 DEPARTMENT OF HEALTH AND SOCIAL SECURITY *Social Security Statistics 1987* London, HMSO, 1987.

7 GOLDING P. and MIDDLETON S. *Images of welfare. Press and public attitudes to poverty* Oxford, Martin Robertson, 1982.

8 HARRISON P. *Inside the inner city* Harmondsworth, Penguin, 1983.

9 HEDGES A. and RITCHIE J. *Designing documents for people: a report on research carried out for the Department of Health and Social Security's Document Design Unit* London, Social and Community Planning Research, 1988.

10 KERR S. *Making ends meet. An investigation into the claiming of supplementary pensions* London, Bedford Square Press, 1983.

11 McDONAGH T. *Final report of the Haringey rent allowance study* London, Department of the Environment, nd.

12 MEACHER M. *Rate rebates: a study of the effectiveness of means tests* London, Child Poverty Action Group, 1972.

13 PAGE D. and WEINBERGER B. *The take up of rent rebates and allowances in Birmingham* Birmingham, Centre for Urban and Regional Studies, 1975.

14 RITCHIE J. and ENGLAND J. *The Hackney benefit study* London, Social and Community Planning Research, 1988.

15 RITCHIE J. and MATTHEWS A. *Take up of rent allowances: an in-depth study* London, Social and Community Planning Research, 1982.

16 TARPEY M. *English speakers only* London, Islington People's Rights Action Research Project, 1984.

17 TAYLOR-GOOBY P. *Means-testing and social policy* Unpublished MPhil Thesis, University of York, 1974.

18 TAYLOR-GOOBY P. 'Rent benefits and tenants' attitudes. The Batley rent rebate and allowance study' *Journal of Social Policy* 5, 1976, 33–48.

19 WALKER R. Personal Communication.

DHSS RESEARCH REPORT SERIES

No. 1	Advisory and Counselling Services for Young People, 1978	Mary Tyler
No. 2	Community Homes: A Study of Residential Staff, 1978	Pat Cawson
No. 3	Towards Participation: A study of self-management in a Neighbourhood Community Centre, 1978	Dione Crousaz Carolyn Davies Andrea Weston
No. 4	Fatherless Families on Family Income Supplement (FIS), 1979	J Nixon
No. 5	Children Referred to Closed Units, 1979	Pat Cawson Mary Martell
No. 6	Families, Funerals and Finances: A study of funeral expenses and how they are paid, 1980	P J Hennessy
No. 7	The Impact of the Mobility Allowance: An evaluative study, 1981	Kenneth R Cook Frances M Staden (University of York SPRU)
No. 8	Social Work: A Research Review, 1981	Dione Crousaz
No. 9	Local Authority Community Work: Realities of Practice, 1983	Carolyn Davies Dione Crousaz
No. 10	The Classification and Measurement of Disability, 1983	Derek Duckworth
No. 11	For Richer, for Poorer? DHSS Cohort Study of Unemployed Men, 1984	S Moylan J Millar R Davies
No. 12	Costs and Benefits of the Heart Transplant Programmes at Harefield and Papworth Hospitals, 1985	Martin Buxton Roy Acheson Noreen Caine Stuart Gibson Bernie O'Brien
No. 13	The Medical Effects of Seat Belt Legislation in the United Kingdom, 1985	William Rutherford Tony Greenfield H R M Hayes J K Nelson
No. 14	Re-establishment and Rehabilitation of the Long-term Unemployed	R A Abel H Houghton S Buckland
No. 15	Teenage Mothers and Their Partners	Madeleine Simms Christopher Smith

Printed in the United Kingdom for Her Majesty's Stationery Office
Dd290972 7/88 C10 G443 10170